God Is Beautiful, Man

D1287906

Books by Carl F. Burke

GOD IS BEAUTIFUL, MAN
GOD IS FOR REAL, MAN
TREAT ME COOL, LORD

God Is Beautiful, Man

Interpretations of Bible passages and stories, as told by some of God's bad-tempered angels with busted halos to **Carl F. Burke**

ASSOCIATION PRESS ⌃ NEW YORK

God Is Beautiful, Man

SBN: Cloth edition 8096-1713-7
Paperback edition 8096-1720-X

Library of Congress catalog card number: 69-18841

"At the Door" from *Prayers,* by Michel Quoist,
© Sheed & Ward Inc., 1963

PRINTED IN THE UNITED STATES OF AMERICA

At The Door

The boy stumbled on the landing and the door
slammed behind him.
He had been punished.
Suddenly aware of his disgrace, he rushed in anger
at the unfeeling door.
He slapped it, pounded it, stamping and shriek-
ing.
But on the wooden surface not a fiber moved.
The boy caught sight of the keyhole—ironic eye
of that sullen door—
But on peering into it he saw that it was blocked.
Then, in despair, he sat down and cried.

I watched him, smiling, and realized, Lord, that
often I exhaust myself before locked doors.
I want to make my points, convince, prove,
And I talk and brandish arguments,
I strike hard to reach the imagination or the
emotions,
But I am politely or violently dismissed—I waste
my strength, vain fool that I am.

Grant, Lord, that I may learn to wait reverently,
Loving and praying in silence,
Standing at the door till it is opened.

from PRAYERS by Michel Quoist

To John F. Burke
and
Lillian M. Burke

Contents

Why This Book 11

The First Rub-Out 20
   Cain and Abel (Genesis 4)

Joe's Daydream 22
   Joseph as a Dreamer (Genesis 37)

Joe's Brothers' Dirty Trick 25
   Joseph and His Brothers (Genesis 42-45)

Joe and Ben 30
   Joseph and Benjamin (Genesis 43:1-44:13)

Joe Shows Who He Was 34
   How Joseph Revealed Himself (Genesis 45)

Moses' People Go on a Trip 36
   The Exodus (Exodus 13:15-15:3)

How Moses' People Got Food 39
   God Provides Manna (Exodus 15:22-16:35)

The Stick and the Rock 40
   The Rock at Horeb (Exodus 17:1-6)

The Lord's My Man 42
   (Psalm 27)

Wishing God Was Around 42
   (Psalm 84)

Listen to the Teach', Man 43
   Brief selections from the Proverbs

There Is a Guy Comin' 46
   The Suffering Servant (Isaiah 53)

The Busted Fence 47
   The Walls of Jericho (Joshua 5:13-6:25)

Dan Reads the Wall **48**
    The Writing on the Wall (Daniel 5:1-31)

Dan Gets Dragged **50**
    Daniel in the Lion's den (Daniel 6:1-9:27)

When Jesus was a Little Cat **52**
    The Boyhood of Jesus

Preaching on a Hill **54**
    The Sermon on the Mount (Matthew 5-7)

Groovy Things **59**
    Miracles of Jesus

A Girl Who Was Sick **61**
    The Daughter of Jairus (Mark 5:22-43)

The Guy at the Pond **62**
    The Waters of Bethesda (John 5:1-6)

The Funeral **64**
    The Son Who Was Dead (Luke 7:11-17)

Who Is This Guy? **65**
    Jesus Calms the Sea (Mark 4:37-41)

Fishin' **65**
    The Lowering of the Nets (Matthew 4:18-22)

Nutty Things **67**
    The Hidden Treasure (Matthew 13:44)

A Real Young Bread Man **67**
    Jesus and the Rich Man (Matthew 19:16-30)

Watch Out, You Jokers and Hipes **70**
    The Scribes and Pharisees (Matthew 23:13-23)

Five Stupid, Five Hep **71**
    The Ten Virgins (Matthew 25:1-13)

Spooks—Get Out! **72**
    Casting out Evil Spirits (Mark 1:23-26)

How About That? **74**
    Walking on the Water (Mark 6:45-52)

The Loan Sharks **75**
    The Story of the Money Changers (Mark 11:15-19)

A Tree in the Park **76**
    The Unfruitful Tree (Luke 13:6-9)

The Panhandler **77**
    The Blind Beggar (Luke 18:35-43)

Thanks, Man **78**
    Healing the Lepers (Luke 17:11-19)

Settling a Mess **79**
    Jesus and Little Children (Mark 10)

A Cool Wedding **81**
    The Wedding at Cana (John 2:1-11)

A Creep Makes It **82**
    Nicodemus (John 3:1-15)

Like, great, Man **84**
    The Samaritan Woman (John 4:4-12)

Big Parade **86**
    The Palms (John 12)

Don't Forget Me **87**
    The Last Supper (John 13:1-38)

Don't Get Shook Up **91**
    In My Father's House (John 14:1-12)

After Jesus Busts out of the Grave **92**
    Jesus Appears (John 20:1-21:24)

Saul Gets Turned Around **93**
    Saul's Conversion (Acts 9:1-9)

Getting Sins Fixed Up **95**
    (Acts 10:34)

Tell 'Em Off **96**
(Acts 28:26)

Paul Writes to the Cats in Rome **97**
Letter to the Romans

Listen, Brother **98**
Life as a Christian (Romans 12)

How to Treat Another Guy **100**
(Romans 13:8-14)

Love Letter **101**
The Way of Love (I Corinthians 13)

God's Gonna Stick by You **103**
(Philippians)

Real Strong Like God **104**
The Armor of God (Ephesians 6:10-20)

Lazy Bums **104**
Idleness (II Thessalonians 3:6-15)

They All the Same **105**
Show No Partiality (James 2:1-13)

Adam and His Wife **107**
A Play About the Garden of Eden (Genesis)

Jonah, You're My Man **110**
A Play About Jonah and the Whale (Jonah)

A Christmas Play **116**

Cool Yule **118**

Glossary **126**

Why This Book

As a result of *God Is for Real, Man* and *Treat Me Cool, Lord*, I have received a vast number of letters and other forms of communication. Most have been favorable; a surprisingly small number have been critical. One of the criticisms has been that the books produced laughter. Some people went so far as to say that humor has no place in biblical or religious teaching. Another kind of comment, questioning if not critical, has had to do with how the books were written. People have asked about the techniques of encouraging young people, particularly those who are delinquent or in jail, to participate in biblical paraphrasing.

I am in no position to argue with those who accuse the paraphrases of being humorous, because they are. At points they are just plain funny. No apologies are made for this quality. If experience in a jail setting has taught me anything, it is the validity of humor—indeed, the importance of humor—in conveying and teaching basic religious concepts. Many of the young people I work with come from disadvantaged homes. The reality of just existing from one day to another has created problems which many of us cannot imagine. Their situations produce tensions and fears that close off communication, especially within the religious realm.

In the introduction to *Ecumania,* a book edited by Hiley Ward, three American comedians offer some observations which apply in the teaching of religious values. Danny Thomas says, "Laughter dispels ignorance, ignorance begets fear which begets hatred and when laughter dispels ignorance it rules out fear."

If one can understand that often the young people involved with me in these paraphrases are filled with hostilities, resentments, rejection, and hatred, and that laughter actually does dispel these feelings, perhaps it will help the reader to accept the humor.

Myron Cohn, another comedian, writes, "Humor opens lines of communication. It not only stirs positive emotions but it can get attention, which is important in communications." Those of us who are active in the field of the communication of religious values would not deny the difficulty of getting the attention of people and maintaining that attention. And who would deny that laughter is a positive emotion?

And Godfrey Cambridge puts his finger on one of the major problems that we face when he said, "Humor helps to break down tensions in society." Frequently it is the tensions which destroy communication of religious values.

So my contention is that humor can be the avenue by which a young person can find himself, but more importantly by which he can find God. Of course, when one uses humor as a method of

GOD IS BEAUTIFUL, MAN

teaching in the area of religion, it ought not be just for the sake of being funny or cute, but rather with the realization that it is a gift of God. It is an important tool which religious leaders need to rediscover.

By far, the question asked most frequently about the books that come out of my work is, how do you get the young people to participate in biblical paraphrasing? Some people have indicated that the books were "phony", so great was their disbelief, their lack of comprehension of the feelings of people who are socially deprived or disadvantaged. The lack of any encounter with people outside of their own class structure truly does make it impossible for such critics to comprehend the feelings of others. They need to develop contacts that will reveal emotions and longings and a search for God. They need to discover, for example, that children from the so-called "tough parts" of a city ask questions that can be built on. For instance, a city child who has been given a chance to go to a summer camp asks why God made mosquitos—a rainbow—hills. There is a natural inquisitiveness, and if one is not preachy in his response, he has an opening. It is important to respond to a simple question so that it will give rise to more questions.

Actually, I have no formula for involving young people in this work with the Bible that is not readily available in the concept of dialogue and the material that has been written about it. There is of course the necessity of becoming thoroughly familiar with the persons you are associating with. One must have respect for them as persons—as children of God—and for the validity of their viewpoints.

A communication gap exists between socioeconomic groupings. The disbelief expressed by middle-income citizens is actually the same disbelief expressed by people of lower income status. To some extent it reveals how little we are aware of the various value structures, the argot, and the frames of reference of others. It also reveals that there are those in all cultures who respond to a religious message and those who do not.

One of the barriers in the communication of religious values is that of language. The very words that we use are influenced by the experiences that we have been subjected to. Therefore, meanings that we give to words are frequently far different than the meanings given to the same words by another group. For example, to the kids I know the word "kite" is a written message on a piece of paper which is smuggled from one inmate to another or smuggled to a person on the outside. If someone from the middle class is going to communicate effectively with a disadvantaged city kid, particularly about Christian concepts, he's going to have to know and use the language forms of the kids of the street.

Much biblical terminology is agrarian, but many of the young people with whom I work come from an inner city where sheep are seldom seen, if ever. It is difficult in a jail setting to talk about babbling brooks and hills and grains of wheat or "amber waves of grain." The natural and familiar images for the child of the streets are high rise apartments, broken street lights, and winos. Talking with him about religion effectively means to use urban settings and everyday experiences.

Much of the paraphrasing in these books was done by young people in jail or detention homes. One of the greatest enemies of a person so confined is boredom. This boredom can become so overpowering that a youngster will try anything to break it up—even trying to paraphrase the Bible. Some of the kids I work with participate for this reason—which, in reality, is not far removed from the reasons why other kids go to Sunday school. For other young people, to participate in the paraphrasing is only a "blast" that never seems to mean anything to them. My feeling about such a relationship is that anything that will bring about a confrontation with the claims of God is legitimate. Sometimes we are able to go on to a more meaningful relationship, which is actually the ultimate objective of the confrontation.

Obviously, there are still many others in detention who would not participate under any circumstances.

Thus there are varying degrees of participation and involvement. Is this not, however, exactly what we find in a church school situation? A valid conclusion is that, when young people are met at their own level and permitted to respond to guidance, there can be development of communication, acceptance, and interpretation of basic biblical concepts.

Another important point needs to be made. Working with inner city youth, the teacher or leader must see himself and accept himself as he is seen, as a phony. Most clergymen are seen as phonies, as people who do not live in the real world. Many young people in jail setting have only one concept of them, the "goody-goody" men who do not understand the problems that are pressing upon people.

It is not easy to see oneself in this role. Therefore there must be developed within the person an understanding of why he is really interested in others and why he wants to communicate his ideas and the ideas of God. He must also come to an understanding of the value systems and family structures of people he ministers to.

He needs to understand that often when he is being attacked in verbal or nonverbal communication he is actually being tested. The person is attacking to see how he will react and to discover how accepting he can be of the attacker.

If one is to engage in this form of biblical paraphrasing there must be a rather considerable knowledge of the social mores and psychological makeup of the child who is disadvantaged or who is prone to social behavior that will get him in trouble. This knowledge can be secured through study and experience. The latter can be achieved by volunteer service to Christian centers or settlement houses, tutoring programs, and similar activities.

I have found that biblical paraphrasing grows best out of natural situations. For instance, this book contains a retelling of the Sermon on the Mount that developed from a reading in the chapel service of the county jail by one of the inmates. Later in the day, I visited the cell blocks and talked with a group of young men who had attended the service. I asked one of the young men if he understood what had been read from the Bible. His response was that he "didn't get that jazz." A little probing revealed that he was not certain what was meant by the words, "If salt has lost its taste, how shall its saltness be restored?" We discussed salt and pepper as spices that give a better taste to our food. One of the young men spoke up and said, "You mean like the stuff we put on hamburgers." A hamburger for these young men was part of their daily living; they knew what it was like and how unsatisfying a hamburger can be without relish and catsup and mustard added to it. Here a biblical image was translated into a 20th century image. It was also a case of translating all that had been known and learned by the chaplain in the area of dialogue and communication as well as in understanding of the inmates. In this exchange a point of understanding had been achieved. It was a base upon which we could build.

The words, the thought pattern, the frame of reference don't really count; it is the message that is important. In all the paraphrasing that we have done, I have insisted that one very important rule be followed: Under no circumstances can we change the meaning of the message.

The paraphrases in *God Is Beautiful, Man* are, except for spelling, changed little if at all from the way they were expressed. I would have left the spelling uncorrected if it had not threatened to distract from the impact that the work of the young people can make upon us.

Although paraphrasing the Scriptures is not new, the forms it takes in this book may be shocking to some. We have surrounded our religious values with the niceties of life in speech and manners. We have built majesty and grandeur into our cathedrals, perhaps inhibiting people from involvement. But Christianity in its early stages was an earthy faith. There are many examples of Christ meeting people at their own level. His method was to lead.

One final point: Hero stories play a major part in the development of the character of many men. For the boys with whom I work, the hero concept is expressed frequently by admiration for the president of some anti-social gang. This tendency indicates that Christian education should make use of hero stories. For that reason, this book has stories of Moses and his people and Joseph and his various exploits. Many of the younger boys whose words are found here come from fatherless homes. In some degree and measure, their problems can be attributed to the lack of a male image in their lives. It is my belief that the male image is not only lacking in a physical sense but is poorly represented in the abstract by what the boys see on TV and in comic strips. When stories of great men are told, particularly in relationship to the everyday life of the young people, there is noticeable response and interest.

Carl F. Burke
Chaplain, Erie County Jail
Buffalo, New York

The First Rub-Out

Cain and Abel (Genesis 4)

Adam and Eve had two childrens. One got the name Cain and the other got stuck with the name Abel. When they grew up they both got jobs workin' for their parents. Cain gotta job like the guy that cleans up at the city park and fixes up the flowers. They called him a farmer. And Abel gotta job like the guy at the Zoo, takin' care of all the animals.

Even though God kicked Adam outta the garden he still likes him and Adam figured he's still God so he's got the right to do what he wants to do. But just to stay on God's good side, Adam gave him all kinds of stuff that grew in the ground, and sheep and even a few chickens. Now Adam's a pretty good father so he shows Cain and Abel how to stay on the good side of God, too. One day Cain and Abel are out workin' at their jobs and Abel figures that he'd give one of those sheep to God in a thing called a sacrifice. So he put it up on the altar like you see at the front of the church. Now Cain figures that his brother ain't gonna out-do him so he decides he'd make an offering too outta some of the stuff he was growin', like them flowers that grow in the city park. But he really didn't do it 'cause he wanted to, he did it just 'cause he didn't wanta get bested by Abel. Now on account of that, God was happy with Abel's gift but he wasn't really turned on by what Cain did.

GOD IS BEAUTIFUL, MAN

Cain gets pretty bugged about this so God says, "Hey, man, what's buggin' you? If you did what you s'posed to do I'd be pretty happy with you, too." But Cain he's so shook up about this and he don't hear nobody sayin' nothin' and they ain't no point in talkin' to him so he goes over and he starts to chew out Abel. He gets so mad that he belts him one and Abel falls down and Cain stomps on him and kills him. Now that's the first time anybody got killed in the whole world and that's kinda screwy way to start anything too. Then Cain gets shook up even more when he sees what he did. So he figures he better get outta there and make a quick getaway. So he tries to find a pad where he can hide out. Pretty soon he hears God saying, "Hey, Cain, man, where's your brother?" But Cain ain't admittin' nothin'. So he says, "I dunno. Whadda ya think I am, his babysitter or somethin'?" Now God's gettin' kinda mad about this too 'cause he knows that Cain's tryin' to give him a con job. So he says, "Listen, man, I know what's goin' on. You killed your brother and I'm gonna put a hex on you for doin' that. Now—get lost!" And that's what Cain did and everywhere he went he had a rough time and he always felt lousy after that.

One day he was feelin' so bad and really down in the dumps, and he began to bawl, and thinkin' he'd never see anybody he knew, not even God. So he figures there is only one thing to do and that's to go someplace and try to start all over again. So he went to another city and he found a broad and fell in love with her and they got married. But he did pretty good after that. He got a baby and he gave him a screwy name like Enoch, then he built a whole city just like urban renewal and he named the city Enoch. Then he and his wife started havin' kids every year. And the kids started havin' kids every year until there was a whole bunch of them. But the kids did pretty good. Some of them invented music things like guitars and horns and some others invented tools like they use in those gardens. So while Cain had a rough time his kids did pretty good, and at least that part of it was beautiful.

Joe's Daydream

Joseph as a Dreamer (Genesis 37)

There was a guy who had a real big family. His name was Jacob. And the youngest of the cats was a guy named Joseph. And the next youngest was a guy named Benjamin. They were brothers 'cause they had the same mother. The rest of the guys had a different mother so they were only half-brothers. And sometimes this kinda made for a few fights in the house. The other guys began to get the idea that Jacob loved Joseph more than he loved the others and in a way he sorta did. But mostly he loved 'em all. One day all the cats was sittin' around and Joe said to his brothers, "Man,

GOD IS BEAUTIFUL, MAN

did I have a real screwy dream last night. I dreamed that I got to be like a king and all you guys had to bow down in front of me. Well, the brothers don't like that. Then another time Joe has another kinda funny dream. He dreamed that the sun and the moon and the stars had to bow down in front of him. And the brothers began to think that old Joe was gettin' to be some kind of a nut. Then one day Joe told his father about the dream and the father said to him, "Man, you're gettin' too big for yourself. You really think your mother and your father wanta bow down in front of you?"

One day Joseph's brothers all went out in the field to do some work for their old man and they were gone a long time. And the old man began to get worried about 'em. So he sent Joe out to see what was cookin' and where they were. Well it took him a long time to find them but he finally did.

His brothers saw him comin' and they are still pretty shook about him thinkin' he is such a wheel and they even got to talkin' about rubbin' him out but they knew they really wouldn't do that kinda dirty trick. Reuben, the oldest brother, wasn't too hep with Joe either, but anyway he didn't want to kill him. So they figured out they would put him in a big hole in the ground and then let him get out the best way he could, if he could. But really Reuben thought he might come back and get him after the others had gone. Which is kinda sneaky but it's not such a bad thing. So they agreed that's what they'd do. But before they put him in the big hole they took off the coat that he had 'cause it was kinda pretty. Then they all sat down to eat lunch. When they did they saw some other people coming and then one of Joseph's brothers, Judah, said, "They ain't no sense killin' him or leavin' him in the hole. Why don't we sell him and make some money off him? These guys buy slaves and servants and use 'em in Egypt." That seemed like a good idea to everybody except Reuben and he wasn't there. So they did it. And they got the money. But now they got a real big problem. How they gonna tell the old man about this? So this is how they figured it out. They already got Joseph's coat so they killed a goat and they put some of the blood on the coat and they took the coat to the father and then they told their father that a lion or a tiger or something else had killed Joseph. This shook up the old man and he cried and yelled and tore his clothes, he was so sorry that Joseph got killed. But he really didn't. He really got to be a slave, in Egypt. And of all the places to get to be a slave he got to be the slave of the king of Egypt. But Joseph was pretty smart and he won't have nothin' to do with the king's wife who tried to get him into a mess of trouble and the king threw him in the joint for that.

One day one of the king's servants had a real weird dream and Joseph tells him what the dream

GOD IS BEAUTIFUL, MAN

means. Then one day when the Pharaoh had a real screwy dream his servant told him about Joseph in the joint who could tell him what the dreams mean and he did. Well this gets the king to figurin' that Joseph's a pretty smart guy so what does he do? He makes Joseph a real big wheel. And those brothers who figured that they were gonna make a slave outa him got all screwed up because instead of a slave now he ends up the governor of Egypt.

Joe's Brothers' Dirty Trick

Joseph and His Brothers (Genesis 42-45)

Joseph's brothers, the cats that sold him and made him like a slave, didn't know where he was. They had it all figured out that he was dead. So they didn't have to get shook up about him any more.

But things got pretty rough goin' in Canaan where they lived and nobody had much to eat 'cause they was all poor and they didn't have any welfare in those days. One day they needed something to eat real bad like and they was takin' care of their father who was an old man and they had lotsa little kids, and they didn't know what to do. So they was just lookin' at each other and then their father says to them, "Well, don't just stand there, man, do somethin'!" And he tells them that they got plenty stuff down in Egypt and they'd better go down there and buy some flour so they can make bread, instead of standin' there and starvin'. So they decide that's what they better do and they left Ben behind to take care of the old man.

Well, when these characters get to Egypt they discover that there's cats from all over the world there, 'cause everybody's poor and the only place that anything's been growin' is in Egypt, which is kinda groovy too.

But a real groovy thing happened. Who do you s'pose was the governor of Egypt? Joseph! When his brothers get there they go walkin' up to the governor and they get down on their hands and knees and they put their faces in the earth. Well now, they didn't recognize Joseph but he figures out who they are, only he acts out like he don't know it. So Joseph, he says, "Where did you guys come from?" and they says, "We come from Canaan, we wanta buy some flour. We hear you got plenty government surplus stuff." They still don't know this is Joseph. So he decides he's gonna bug 'em a little bit so he yells at 'em, "I know who you guys are, you're spies. You came down here to check us out and see if we would be easy push-overs for you." Well, the brothers, they say, "Oh, you got us all wrong, governor, we ain't spies. We just wanta get some flour, so that nobody in our family is gonna starve to death."

Joseph is still making out like he didn't know who they were or believe them, so he just kept callin' them spies and they just kept sayin' that they wasn't. But Joseph he didn't speak that way 'cause he was angry. He just wanted to make sure they wouldn't know who he was. 'Cause he was gonna be pretty good to them. And he kind of knew this but he just wanted to put on a little show. So then they says to him, "We are all brothers and we gotta father that had twelve sons and one of them is still with the father up in Canaan and his name is Ben." And one they said was dead. They kind of figured that would make the governor feel sorry for them. Well, Joe, he just kinda laughs a little inside him and he still pretends he don't believe them. So he said, "I gotta check you guys out and see if you're tellin' the truth." And he said, "This is the way you gotta do it. One of you has gotta go back home and bring the youngest kid here and all of the rest of you have to stay here." So to make sure they stayed there, he put them in the joint for three days. Then on the third day Joseph had his brothers brought out of the joint and he said to them, "Well, all of you can go back home, except one." And the ones that was going back home could take some flour so they could make some bread to eat. But one of the brothers had to stay in the joint so that Joseph would be sure that the others would come back, and bring the youngest guy with them. Well, the brothers, when they heard this, figured out that Joe really meant what he was sayin' only they didn't know he was Joe, for they thought he was the governor. And this kinda bugs them inside. Then it starts to get to them that maybe God was gettin' even with them for selling their brother so long ago. And they began to talk with each other about it and they figured out they had been pretty rotten to do a trick like that. One of the brothers, the oldest, his name was Reuben. It was Reuben who really wanted to save Joseph so long ago when they threw him in that hole in the ground. So he says, "Didn't I tell you guys we shouldn't have done that? And you talked me into it. Now look what's happening. You guys wouldn't listen to me. Now we are in a peck of trouble and it's all because of you."

Joe heard them talking and figuring these things out, and they kept talking because they didn't know that he could understand what they said. They didn't know he could speak the same language. They figured he only could speak the Egypt language, 'cause that was all he spoke to them, and even then he had to have a guy that spoke Egyptian and Hebrew too. While this was goin' on, Joseph's feeling pretty good about it inside. So he had to get out of there so they wouldn't see him laughin' at 'em. But it was the kind of laughin' that made him cry too. Then a little while later he came back to talk to them. But he still made them think that he thought they were spies. Then he took Simon, one of the brothers, and he put him in the joint and the rest saw him do it, 'cause Simon had to stay in Egypt

GOD IS BEAUTIFUL, MAN

while all of the other guys went home to get Ben, and to bring him back.

So then Joe, he does a real groovy thing. He tells the guys that work in the flour mill to fill up the bags that the brothers brought and then to sneak the money back in with the flour when they didn't know it. That was on account of Joe didn't think it was right to take money to take care of your own family. So then when everything was all ready they started back home. Well, on the way home they stopped at like a gin mill to get somethin' to eat and they looked in the bags and they saw the money. Well this gets the brothers all jammed up, 'cause they didn't know who put the money there or how it got there. So they decided they'd better get home in a hurry. And when they got there they told their father the things that had happened to them—about how the governor thought they were spies and how he really chewed them out because he thought they were enemies. They told their father how they tried to tell him they weren't spies, that they were all brothers and how he was testing them to find out if they were telling the truth and how they had to bring Ben back and if they didn't they wouldn't get Simon and they wouldn't get any more flour. But even worse than that, if they didn't, Simon would get plugged.

Then they dumped all the flour out and they discovered that all the money was there. Well, this really gets the father all bugged up and he said,

"You guys are causin' me an awful lotta trouble. First you get Joseph, now you got Simon gone and now they're trying to get Benjamin away." Now he is really mad and stompin' around the house and yellin' and bangin' on the table.

Well, Reuben he has two sons of his own and he thinks he has got a real big deal goin' here. He said, "Well I'll tell you what, Dad, I'll put my two sons down there instead of Benjamin if only I can take Ben to Egypt." And he promised to get him back safely. But the old man is still pretty shook over what he thought was Joseph being dead and now Simon's gone. He says, "What the hell do you want me to do, lose Benjamin too? I couldn't take that." So what happened was that Simon stayed in the joint in Egypt unless they could bring Benjamin. But the old man didn't know what it was all about and he didn't want to take any chances of losin' Benjamin, too.

Joe and Ben

Joseph and Benjamin (Genesis 43:1-44:13)

Things was gettin' even worse for Jacob and his sons. After they made bread outa the flour they got in Egypt and it was all gone, Jacob had to say to the boys again, you better go back down there and get some more flour. Well, one of them says, "Dad, if we go, we gotta take Benjamin with us, otherwise there is no use goin', 'cause the governor said you ain't gonna see me unless your brother is with you." So Jacob says, "What are you guys tryin' to pull on me? What did you have to tell him you got another brother for, anyway?" So they had to level with him and they told him how it happened. They said, "The governor asked us if our father was still alive and kickin', and if we had another brother home, and how did we know anyway that he was gonna tell us that we had to bring our other brother?" So one of the brothers whose name was Judah speaks his piece and he says to his father, "Tell you what, Dad, you better let Ben go and I'll take care of him and if he don't get back you can bust me for it."

Well, Jacob knows things is pretty bad and they either got to take the chance or starve to death so he said, "OK, but tell you what we'll do. You take along some of the food we got and some of the honey and this other stuff and some money and you better take back the money that was in those bags and then take your brother and go back down to that guy and see what you can do."

Now Jacob ain't takin' no chances so he has a little prayer meeting for the kids right there 'cause he didn't want to be lonely any more and didn't want any more kids taken away from him. So then they all starts off for Egypt with the presents and the money and this time they got Ben with them. And when they gets there, they goes right in to see Joe. But they don't know who he is, they still think he is the governor. Then Joe says to one of the servant guys, "Take these men and bring them all over to my house. I'm gonna have a drink with 'em and eat dinner with 'em." Well, the brothers are gettin' real scared now 'cause they think they're gonna get blamed for that money that they took back. They think that the governor thinks they stole it and they're gonna end up as slaves. So when they get to Joe's house they start talkin' to one of the servants, thinking they can cool it with him, and that he'll put in a good word for 'em and get 'em off the hook. Well the servant said, "Can it, man, ain't nothin' gonna happen to you." Just about that time Simon who got outta the joint came and met his brothers, and man, were they ever glad to see him. Then the servant took 'em all upstairs and they got all washed up for dinner. Well then Joe comes back in and they still think he's the governor and they gave him a present and they bowed their faces down to the earth again. Well then Joe speaks real nice like and he says, "Is your father OK, is he still alive?" And they said, "Yeah, he's OK." Then they bowed their faces down to the earth again. Then Joe spies his brother Benjamin and he said, "Oh, is this young guy, the brother, that you talked about?"

Well, old Joe can't stand it no more. He's gettin' all choked up so he beats it into his bedroom and bawls his eyes out, not because he was sad but because he was so happy. You see Benjamin was the only real full brother he had, the others

GOD IS BEAUTIFUL, MAN

was only half-brothers. Then he washed his face so that nobody would know he had been bawlin'. When it came time to eat, Joseph had the places set just right so that the oldest brother would have the first seat and the next oldest the next, and stuff like that. Well this kinda gets the brothers all shook up again because they begins to wonder, "How do you know how old we are?" Then when Joe sent the food to the brothers he sent a lot more to Benjamin. And even though they were all eatin' together, even though they were at different tables, they still were not hep as to who Joseph was.

Well then Joe told his servant to fill the guys' sacks up with food, as much as they could carry, and to put every man's money back in the bag just like they did before. Then he said, "Put my cup in the bag of the youngest one." So that's just what the servant did. And then the brothers start back to Canaan. When they left the city they didn't go very far when Joe told his servant to follow them and to nail them for takin' that silver cup. So he did. Well the brothers were pretty spooked when they discovered what that servant wanted. And they said, "We wouldn't snitch your master's cup. Don't you remember we even told you we brought the money back. We coulda kept it if we wanted to but we didn't. So why would we steal a cup?" So then the servant says, "I tell you what. The one that's got the cup is gonna be my servant and the rest of you won't get blamed." So they searched in the bags and sure enough Benjamin had the cup. But they got real mad about it but they wouldn't let Benjamin go. No matter what that servant said, they weren't gonna turn over another one of their sons to them Egyptians, and that's for sure.

Joe Shows Who He Was

How Joseph Revealed Himself (Genesis 45)

When the brothers all came back to Joe's house, he was still there, and they still didn't know who he was. Which must mean they was pretty dumb. So they bowed down and put their heads in the ground like they had been always doin'. Old Joe is still makin' out like he don't know who they are and he is still makin' out like he thinks they stole the cup. So he says, "Didn't you guys know I'd find you out?" Well Judah is the head man and so he says, "Whatta we gonna do, are we gonna be your servants?" And Joe said, "Only one of you had the cup so he's gonna be my slave. The rest of you can go back to your old man." So then Judah says, "Can I say somethin'?" Joe says, "Fire away." So then Judah says, "Governor, you remember how you asked us if we had a brother at home and a father and we told you we did? Well, our father loves this boy that you made us bring back and I guess he especially loves him because he has got a brother

GOD IS BEAUTIFUL, MAN

who's dead and his mother's dead and if we don't bring him back with us our father might get kicked off too. So we can't go, and we ain't goin' unless Benjamin is with us." And then Judah says, "And besides I promised I'd take the blame so why can't I stay and be your slave and let Ben go home and then nothin' will happen to the old man?"

Old Joe can't take it no longer, so he tells all of his servants to get the hell outta the room so no one's left in that room but Joe and his brothers. And he is so choked up that he starts cryin', and then he says, "Don't you guys know it? I'm really Joseph. Is it really true that Pop's still alive?" Well the brothers figure this is some kind of a game and they don't really believe him. So then he says, "Come near me." And they did. And he says, "Don't you recognize me? I'm your brother, the one that you sold."

So he tells them not to get too shook up about it 'cause things worked out pretty good and that it musta been part of God's plan so that he could be there and keep them from starvin'. But Joseph didn't really mean they did the right thing when they sold him. He just meant that God made a good thing out of it. And maybe he told them that so they wouldn't be too shook up and afraid. 'Cause he really loved them and he kinda wanted them to say they was sorry too. Then they all starts bawlin' and holdin' each other 'cause they was all so happy. So then Joe he takes over again and he tells them to go back to Canaan and tell their father Jacob that God made Joe ruler over all of Egypt and that if he didn't want to starve to death he had better come on down there, and that Joe would take good care of him. Then when that was all taken care of Joe grabbed his brother Benjamin 'cause he was so glad to see him and he started doin' all those screwy things like kissin' and huggin'. So then the brothers they all went back to Canaan. They had plenty of flour this time and when they got back, man, were they ever glad with the news they had for their father. Even then he didn't believe it when he heard that his son was the governor of Egypt and old Jacob was so glad he said he would go to Egypt right away and see his son before he died, and you better believe he did!

Moses' People Go on a Trip

The Exodus (Exodus 13:15-15:3)

Moses' people were slaves in Egypt. There was a real rotten king there, his name was Pharaoh. Moses had fixed up a big deal with the Pharaoh so his people could go back to their own turf. Then Pharaoh got so scared he said they could go. Well this all comes as a big surprise to Moses' people. They ain't packed up and the movin' vans didn't come and they didn't even have a lunch packed. Now Pharaoh's idea is to have these people get lost quick. Get outta sight. Take

GOD IS BEAUTIFUL, MAN

off. Go, baby, go! So some of Moses' mothers mixed up some dough like that they was gonna make pizzas to take along. Pharaoh's people wants 'em to go. So they gave 'em some gold and some jewels so they could stop at hot dog stands along the way or somethin'.

Now Moses' people figures they'd go back to their home in Canaan, that's sort of north like, but maybe they wanted to fool old Pharaoh's gang so they didn't take the short cut. But more than that there was some big guys called Philistines who didn't like nobody on their turf and Moses' people didn't want to get into any more trouble so they decided to go around it. First they took a trip to a place that looked like a state park on the edge of a big sandy desert. And they made like a camp. There was a real crazy thing goin' on too. They didn't know the way to go so God sent a cloud and they followed the cloud. It was a kind of a funny lookin' cloud, it looked like a big fat log like you see floatin' in the lake. And in the daytime it was white and in the night time it looked like it was on fire. So they just followed it and you don't have to believe it if you don't want to.

Well, old Pharaoh he has got a real hang up now 'cause he said these people could go but now he's got nobody to be his slaves and nobody to do his work so he says to his guys, "We better go get them and bring them back." So he gets all his people and they go out to make a war, and that's the kinda thing that makes him a rotten king. And man, did he ever mean to do those Moses' people in but good!

But Moses' people are still camped in the state park and when Pharaoh started gettin' near the Israelites heard about it and that made 'em real mad and they started hangin' the bag on Moses for it. And they said it would'a been better for us to stay and work than to get knocked off here in the desert. But Moses says, "All right you guys, pipe down. Nothin's gonna happen. Wait and see how God's gonna take care of us. 'Cause something is gonna happen and you'll never see these guys again."

Well, about that time another funny thing starts happening. That cloud moved and got behind Moses' people and made light so Moses' people could see. Then God says to Moses, "Tell your people to move out and you lift up that stick you got in your hand and hold it out over the water. Then you and your people can walk on the dry ground." Well this sounds kinda screwy to Moses, too. But he thought he'd give it a fling anyway and about that time the wind blew and whatta you know! The water moved away and there was dry ground. So Moses' people walked down in it and right across the seas and the water was piled up on both sides but even then they wuz a little scared about it.

Well this makes old Pharaoh really teed off. So he gets his army and he says, "Get 'em." His peo-

GOD IS BEAUTIFUL, MAN

ple starts in on the dry ground, then a real wild thing happened, the wheels come off of the chariots and the Egyptians are really gettin' bugged about it and one of them says, "Hey, we better get outta here." But before they could, God told Moses, "Pull out that stick again." And Moses did and the water all came back and all that rotten Pharaoh's army got drowned. And that's how Moses' people got outta Egypt.

How Moses' People Got Food

God Provides Manna (Exodus 15:22-16:35)

Well after Moses and his people got outta Egypt and through that scary thing in the water, they're in another desert and there was no water there, except some which was polluted. So they started gripin' to Moses, "Whatta we gonna drink, man?" Well Moses didn't know what to do so he decided that he would pray. And God showed him a tree and he took it and he threw it in the water and all the crud went outta the water and they could drink it. And after that they had enough water. But then Moses gets more troubles. These cats are hungry now and that makes them feel mad. They start cussin' out Moses, sayin' things like, "We used to have plenty to eat, now we ain't even got government surplus stuff." Then they even get screwy ideas like Moses brought 'em there so they could drop dead. But God is still on Moses' side and he tells Moses, "If these cats'll just shut up for the night, in the mornin' there'll be plenty to eat."

Sure enough, in the mornin' birds come by — sorta like hens, — so they had a chicken dinner. Then in the mornin' too there was white stuff all over the ground, it looked like pancakes. But they didn't know what it was 'cause they really didn't have pancakes in them days. So Moses says, "This is the stuff you're gonna eat. Get all you need, but don't take more than that, 'cause it might get rotten and you'll get a guts ache if you eat it." But they didn't really believe him so some of the people took too much and it got maggots in it. So after that they get wised up and then they only go out and get what they need, except on Saturday, when they pick up enough of that stuff for two days and wonder how it didn't get maggots then. And that's how they got enough stuff to eat, while they were takin' the trip back to their home turf.

The Stick and the Rock
The Rock at Horeb (Exodus 17:1-6)

On the trip of Moses' people back to their own turf they kept gettin' into all kinds of messes. And every time they did they started chewin' out Moses. They got in more trouble 'cause they didn't have any water to drink, and they started yellin', "Give us some more water, we're thirsty." "What did you bring us to this place for?"

GOD IS BEAUTIFUL, MAN

Moses is gettin' a little fed up with this and he probably wanted to tell 'em to knock it off and shut up. But he didn't. He just said, "Why don't you trust God a little more?" But they didn't. They just got madder and madder and this gets Moses even more scared, in fact he got so scared that he went away and prayed a little about what they supposed to do. So God tells Moses, "See that big mountain over there? Well you start goin' towards that mountain," and Moses did. When he got there he found a great big rock even bigger than the ones down on the break wall. Then he took that stick he was always carryin' and he took a poke at the rock and sure enough, there was like a spring in it and water came out and they got a drink. But that's not the end of the lousy mess, 'cause by the time they got the drink there was a big rumble brewin'. The Israelites set up a big crash pad and there was another gang that didn't like it and they decided they would have a real big rumble with these Moses people. So Moses goes and he gets a guy named Joshua and he said, "You pick out the big guys and go out and knock off those Ammocites." Moses went up on a big hill where he could watch the whole battle. And he held up his hands and that stick so his people would know he was still around and that God was with them. And sure enough Moses' people won the rumble and after that they didn't have too much more trouble until they got back to their own turf.

The Lord's My Man
Psalm 27

The Lord is my man. When he's around I'm scared a nothin'. When the hoods and my enemies come to get me he knocks 'em down. When a whole buncha them come I'm not afraid either 'cause I got a good feelin' in me. There's only one thing I really want and that's always to have God around me and me around him. Then when things get real rough he'll stick by me and be real solid. Then I can be real cool and maybe even sing a couple of songs for him. Then sometimes when I get to feelin' real low I can hunt for God and he'll hear me and I'll find him 'cause he won't be very far away. Then when Mom and Pop maybe get on a drunk God will be with me. Then God will learn me his ways and make sure nothin' goes too bad for me. And if I didn't believe that I'd give up. It's good to wait for God and to have real heart and to always know he's around.

Wishing God Was Around
Psalm 84

You got a real nice house, man, and I keep wishin' I could play in your backyard. And when I think about it I feel funny all over me. Sometimes I think about the birds havin' a nest in the top of the buildings and about how you care about them and I remember how big you are. And sometimes I think about people in your house and how happy they are so I guess it's not havin' such a big house but knowin' that you are around to help us even when we are in scary places. So we hope you will hear us and that you'll give a look at us 'cause we know that you are around. It's sure better to spend a day with you than to get locked up and it's sure better to shine shoes for a nickel than to get a year and a nickel at the pen. God, you're real beautiful, and we're sure glad you're around when we are makin' the scene so that we will have everything we need. And we are glad you can like us.

Listen to the Teach', Man

Brief selections from the Proverbs

Trust in the Lord with all your heart
    and do not rely on your own insight.
In all your ways acknowledge him,
    and he will make straight your paths.

(Proverbs 3:5-6)

Have a good feeling with God
    and not with yourself.
        Act like he wants you to.
            You'll come out right, mano!

*   *   *

A wise son makes a glad father,
    but a foolish son is a sorrow to his mother.

(Proverbs 10:1)

A cool son makes a cool father,
   a punk makes a sad mother.

                *   *   *

The way of a fool is right in his own eyes,
   but a wise man listens to advice.
The vexation of a fool is right in his own eyes,
   but the prudent man ignores an insult.

                              (Proverbs 12:15-16)

A nut always figures he's right
   A smart guy plays it cool
A nut's got a low boil
   A smart guy just walks away.

                *   *   *

He who walks with wise men becomes wise,
   but the companion of fools will suffer harm.

                              (Proverbs 13:20)

Hang around with the right gang—
   You're in
Hang around with the wrong gang—
   You've had it man!

                *   *   *

A soft answer turns away wrath,
   but a harsh word stirs up anger.   (Proverbs 15:1)

A cool answer cools people down
   A blast gets you a belt in the mouth.

                *   *   *

Pride goes before destruction,
   and a haughty spirit before a fall.

                              (Proverbs 16:18)

A blowhard is soon messed up
   and a Mr. Big is soon on the bottom of things.

*   *   *

He who is slow to anger is better than the mighty,
   and he who rules his spirit than he who takes
      a city.   (Proverbs 16:32)

You ain't weak if you don't get mad quick,
It's better to watch yourself than be mayor.

*   *   *

Even a child makes himself known by his acts,
   whether what he does is pure and right.
The hearing ear and the seeing eye,
   the Lord has made them both. (Proverbs 20:11-12)

A cat gets known by his acts
   good—or bad,
And the Lord don't miss any of it.

*   *   *

Every way of a man is right in his own eyes,
   but the Lord weighs the heart.   (Proverbs 21:2)

Everybody thinks he's right
   but God's the judge, man.

*   *   *

A good name is to be chosen rather than
     great riches,
   and favor is better than silver and gold.
(Proverbs 22:1)

Better to have a good rep
   than lots of bread.

GOD IS BEAUTIFUL, MAN   · 45 ·

There Is a Guy Comin'

The Suffering Servant (Isaiah 53)

You probably won't believe this 'cause it's kinda hard.

There's a guy comin' that sure won't look like much and maybe even kinda funny like the plant that grows up between the cracks in the sidewalk that don't look like much at all.

He may even look like the winos that falls down on the sidewalk and nobody pays no attention to them.

But like the winos he's gonna know what it is to feel sad and like nobody wants you and that nobody 'll even look at you and we'll make believe we didn't even see him.

But he will be carryin' our bag too and he'll know all about how rotten we feel inside of us.

But he got beat on for some of the things we did and stomped on and hit pretty bad, mostly for us so we can be better.

We are all really like the guys in the pen. We all want to do it our way and the Lord put the rap on him.

And even though he was gettin' it he didn't rat on anybody or sound off. He was just like the cows down at the slaughter house, he didn't say anything.

And he got his sentence and he didn't care whether he was with the rich guys or the bad guys.

The Busted Fence

The Walls of Jericho (Joshua 5:13-6:25)

Joshua was the boss man. And one day he was out walkin' around just lookin' things over when he looks up and he sees a real big guy standin' there with his piece in his hands. Now Joshua gets kinda shook up and he says, "Whose side are you on?" The guy looks at Joshua and he says a real groovy thing, that he's a captain in the Lord's army. Then Joshua gets the idea. OK, maybe this guy has come to help him out and that makes him feel pretty good, 'cause he's gotta real problem. Joshua and his people were tryin' to get into the city and they had a big fence around it, and great big gates and they were locked tight. Nobody could go in and nobody could go out.

Now the time comes when Joshua sets up a war plan and it was a real wierdo if there ever was one. This is what it was like: First of all, all the people would walk around the city once every day for six days and the police would go around carryin' religious things and some others would go around blowin' horns and then on the seventh time around they would go around and the police would blow the horns and then they would all start yellin' like hell. And Joshua says that'll make the walls fall down, and that everybody would get killed except people who were in one house. All the gold and silver stuff—nobody was to touch it or they better watch out. Now this war plan did sound kinda weird, maybe some people laughed at it but nothin' else worked so they gave it a try. On the first day they walked around the city and the police blew the horns and they did it every day and maybe the people on the inside figured that the ones on the outside had gone off their rocker. Then came the seventh day and they went around seven times and the horns blew and then everybody yelled like hell. And, bingo, down went the walls. So they shouts, "Beautiful, baby, beautiful!" And Joshua's people went marchin' right in.

Dan Reads the Wall

The Writing on the Wall (Daniel 5:1-31)

One day a guy named Belshar got to be king of a place called Babylon. There was another character named Daniel who lived there and he was supposed to be the smartest guy in the whole world. Well one day this king decides he is going to have a big blast and he invited a thousand people to come over to his pad and have the blast. When they came they had tea cups made outa gold and silver and they drank wine and booze from them. And they began tellin' the king what a great guy he was and how the cups were the best they'd ever seen. Well about halfway through the party a real weirdo thing happened and it scared the hell out of them for it was like a man's

GOD IS BEAUTIFUL, MAN

hands appeared on the wall and started writin' for them. Well they wrote some real weird words and nobody could figure out what they meant. So the king says, "Bring the wise guys here and see if they can figure it out." And soon the wise guys were standing there. And the king says, "If anybody can figure that out I'll give 'em the biggest reward that we got, like a chain to hang around his neck."

Well these wise guys kinda wanted to do what the king wanted them to do 'cause they wanted to be on his side, but they couldn't figure out what was on the wall. So they thought about that guy Daniel. And they said he can even figure out what dreams are saying. So the king sent for Daniel and told him what a big reward he'd get if he could figure it out. But Daniel said, "I don't want nothin' from you, king." Daniel tells the king, "Remember what happened to your father. How God made him a big strong guy and then he turned his back on God and everything went for bust till he got with it again?" "Well," Daniel says to the king, "you know all this and still you don't do what's right, you do as you damn please. You stole them cups from the church and you drunk booze from them, so the words on the wall mean that you been found guilty and you're gonna get a sentence. And your sentence is gonna be that the kingdom is gonna get taken away from you." Now this guy Belshar wasn't takin' no chances so he kept his word about the reward and Daniel got a new suit of clothes and a new chain to wear with his turtle neck sweater and Nehru jacket but that night everything happened. Just as Daniel told 'em it would. For a big army came and beat up all his soldiers and stomped on 'em and the kingdom and another guy got made king.

Dan Gets Dragged
Daniel in the Lion's Den (Daniel 6:1-9:27)

There was a guy named Darius who was the king, and if there was one guy that he was friends with it was Daniel. Daniel was pretty smart. He knew lots of stuff. And besides that he was real cool with everybody. So the king figures here's a guy I better give a good job. So he made him boss of all the priests and everybody else. And the only guy higher than Daniel was the king. This makes the other guys do a real burn and they figures how come the king chose him. And the more they tried to figure it the madder they got, so they decided to find a way to get rid of him, to wipe him out. So they tried to put a contract on him but that didn't work. Then they tried rattin' on him but that didn't work either. And they never could find anything to put the finger on him about.

Then one day they fix up a plan to trap him and get him cut down a bit. So they goes into the king and they butters him up quite a bit and make him feel like he's a bigger man than he really is. They

GOD IS BEAUTIFUL, MAN

gave him a real con job and he didn't even know he was gettin' it. They tells him, "Why not make a law makin' everybody pray to you, and if they pray to anything else you put them in the den of lions for a few days." Well this sounds pretty good to the king and he kinda wanted to be a bigger wheel anyway so he makes the law.

Now these guys knew that Daniel wouldn't pay no never mind to that. So they watch him and put a tailer on him and sure enough they catches him prayin' to God. Then they went in and they ratted to the king about it and they starts yellin' you gotta throw him to the lions. "Throw him to the lions," they yelled.

This makes the king feel bad 'cause he didn't want to throw Dan in the lions' den. And he began to try to think up all kinds of ways he could get out of it. But those rotten guys came back again and kept pushin' him and he couldn't come up with a good alibi so he had to say, "OK, put him in but I gotta speak to him first."

So they brought Daniel and the king says, "Dan, I hate to do this. Maybe your God'll take care of ya." Then the king went home but he didn't sleep none that night. And in the morning he ran like crazy to where the lions were and he yelled in there, "Hey, Daniel, man, you still OK?" He was pretty scared that maybe Daniel wasn't there and that the lions had him for breakfast. But just then a voice came back, "Sure I'm OK. These lions don't want nothin' from me and I don't want nothin' from them and it looks like God took care of me."

Well, this made the king very happy and he yelled to the guards, "Let him outta there." And when Daniel comes out they shook hands and knocked each other around a little bit they was so glad to see each other. Then the king's beginnin' to get wise that he got a con job and he says, "OK, you guys, now it's your turn, get in there." And Daniel got his job back and after the king saw how Daniel was watched out for it was easy for him to believe that God was around to watch out for people.

When Jesus Was a Little Cat
The Boyhood of Jesus

When Jesus was a little cat he lived in a large city on the side of a big hill. Most of their buildins was old and maybe people were talkin' about Urban Renewal or something like that. When you got to the top of the hill you could see a great big lake and a river and there was bridges and boats. And if you got far enough away even the city looked nice.

Jesus grew up in the city so maybe he had a few fights. Maybe he went swimmin' down by the docks. Maybe he was good and strong. Anyway he was pretty smart. The clothes that he wore looked sorta nutty in the pictures or maybe like

GOD IS BEAUTIFUL, MAN

the hippies do now. But that's the kinda stuff that was in then. So it only proves that he was with it and was "real cool."

They didn't have nothin' to do at night then, no youth centers, no coffee houses, no shoes to go out gettin' a job shinin'. So most everybody stayed home and gassed all night. Sometimes people would visit and tell about trips but not the LSD kind. You had a mother and a father which is a pretty good thing to have. Every morning they got up, maybe they had some oatmeal and stuff for breakfast, with even the father there for breakfast. Then they had prayers and stuff like that. They didn't have water in the houses so mothers went with buckets to the mall to get some. And of all the screwy places to carry it, they put it up on their heads. His father was a construction worker, and that's what Jesus got to be too.

Jesus didn't go to school. His mother was his teacher. Then some preachers took over. They all sat on the floor, no desk then. The teacher taught them about God and most of the time they was really friends with each other as they learned all that kind of stuff.

One day they had a Holy Day. Jesus was 12 years old. They took him to a place called Jerusalem. It was a long way and they had to walk and no coke or hot dog stands to stop at either.

When you was 12 in them days, you was grown up and had to go to work. More than that you could get to be a real wheel in a church and tell people what you think and they got to listen too. And they did. And man did Jesus ever spook them with all the stuff he knew. Jesus sure scared his parents one day, his mother and his father that is. They thought he was on the way home but he wasn't. Then they thought he was lost, but he wasn't. Then they thought he was with friends, but he wasn't. He was in the church like preaching and people was listening. But they made him come home and he just got smarter and that's how it was when he was a boy.

Preaching on a Hill
The Sermon on the Mount (Matthew 5-7)

You are like the stuff you put on hamburgers. If it gets so it tastes rotten you can't make it taste good again. So it's no good and gets thrown in the junk bucket and the city dump guys haul it away. You are like a good streetlight. You can't hide it, everybody sees it unless it gets busted. If it's put up on the pole it lights up the whole street. So if you are real cool, people will get the word and be glad that you know God.

If you think I came to ease out what you already got to know you just are not with it, man! I just want you to know that they were for real too!

Grab this man! Nothing, but nothing is gonna get pushed aside as long as there's a world, see!

If you mess up what you got told or them things called commandments you just ain't gonna be much in heaven and when you ain't much there, you just ain't much!

But if you do the best you can and helps other kids do the best they can you got nothing to worry about.

Everybody is always telling you not to kill anybody 'cause you will get found out. But don't ever get mad at some guy—or God will find out. Better not blast them out or swear either. 'Cause that's not safe. You might get cooked in hell. It won't do no good to start praying and things and stuff like that until first you get square with the guy you are mad at or got a contract on. After you and him gets things fixed up you can pray and then it will get through. Even if some one does you in—like getting you put in jail or detention—it's best not to hate him for it.

You heard that you should go out on a date with a pross, but I tell you, you better not even think about it. And if you got something in you that bugs you so much you get into trouble you better get it out. You might end up doing time or have things lousy all your life—or maybe end up in hell—and that don't sound so good.

Then too it's for sure you know you are suppose to keep a promise. Well you is, but watch out how you make it. It's OK to say cross my heart or scouts' oath—and stuff like that. Watch out how you use God's name. It's better to say yes or no and mean it—than to give a lot of snow job promises anyway. You have heard someone say, "I'll get that so and so, or I'll get even with him. Well it's better to cool it no matter what he does (if he don't do it too often). You heard somebody say, I likes some people and hates some people. It's better to love 'em all—even the ones who do you dirt. If you do that you gets to be more like the kinda guy God wants, 'cause he likes everyone. Anyway, man, what's so great about only liking people what likes you—don't take no guts to do that. They is lots of people—even the bad ones—that does it. But God wants you to be better than they is.

When you feels like doing things like praying or counting them beads don't be a show-off. God don't think show-offs is so hot anyway.

When you helps someone out like sharing government surplus stuff, or giving someone some clothes, don't make a big thing out of it. Just do it 'cause you got the stuff, and they ain't and they needs it. Don't let anybody else know about it. You can bet that God knows and that's enough, 'cause he'll take care of you for it.

In your prayers just say what you got on your mind. Never mind all them words that don't mean nothing. God don't care about them long prayers anyway. Here's the way to do it—

God up in heaven

We know even your name is great

We hope your kingdom will get here

And everybody will do what you want
    them to do—just like they do up there.
We hope we'll have enough to feed the whole
    family.
We is sorry if we hurt anyone
    or they hurt us we'll forget it
Don't make things rough for us
    and watch over us
    'cause everything is yours
    and man, are you great
With all kinds of wonderful things about you.

If you don't give on the dirt others did to you,
God won't give on you either—and that's for sure.
But if you do, God will.

And don't go around like a drug freak all day,
or try to make everybody sorry for you. If you are
trying to get right with God, you don't have to
show off. Just some real good thinking and if you
don't feel like eating 'cause you is upset inside,
most of the time nobody cares so why try to show
it off. Anyway they will think you are some kind
of a nut. God will know—and that is what counts.

Don't get too shook up if you ain't rich. Your
money might get lost in a crap game or a mugger
might get it. Put it in the bank, then the muggers
and bank robbers don't have so much of a chance.
But it is better than that to have right ideas about
what you own. Your eyes are like a window. If it's
clean lots of light gets in but if it's got crud and
stuff from the steel mills on it—it's dark inside.

So if there's not much light in you it may be

your own fault and it may be real dark too.

You can't belong to two gangs. You either stand up for one and never have heart for the other. So you gotta be on God's side or on the side of your gang, but not both. It's gotta be one or the other. You make up your mind.

You shouldn't spend so much time trying to be just like other people. So what if they got better clothes than you—who cares anyway, even if they mock you out? The life that God gave you is more important than what you got on. And if you spend a lot of time getting worried about food and clothes and getting turned on you might end up a drug freak or a wino. It's better to do something about it—like knowing God wants you to get busy, you got enough troubles without looking for more.

Don't go around shooting off about people— 'cause God will make up his mind about you too. He will contract you too. Why do you bitch about some guy when you got a problem too? How come you think it's OK to mock out a cat when you're only a phony? First get yourself on the right road. Then you can help a guy.

You don't give a good hot dog to some alley dog, they will only bite you. You don't throw your money in front of a car, you'll get hit.

It's best to ask—then you'll get. Look around and you will find what you're looking for. If you do your share—God does his. If you were a father and had some kids and they was hungry you wouldn't give them a red brick. If you know how

GOD IS BEAUTIFUL, MAN

to give good things, then God does too, and that's for sure. Treat other cats like you want them to treat you. Then you'll get with the ideas of God.

It's easy to follow the gang but hard to have heart and stand up for OK things. But it pays.

Watch careful for big men who think they is something—when they ain't much.

If there is one thing that God don't like it's a phony. So it's no good to say "Lord" if you don't mean it and a snow job is no good either and even a con man won't make it. You will only be told to beat it, you bunch of hoods.

So then if you get the message and get with it you will be pretty smart. You will be like a guy who does a good job of fixing up his heap so it don't break down again. If you don't pay attention to this message you will be like a guy who paid no attention to his heap and it broke down in the traffic, and then he was in a real mess. And all the things Jesus said make lots of sense.

Groovy Things
Miracles of Jesus

Every place that Jesus went he did some real groovy things like fixing up busted bones, or getting sick people better. Every time he did it some people said "Real cool, man!" Some others figured it was a fake and he was a phony. It sure scared the hell out of some too.

Sometimes he touched them, sometimes he yelled at them, sometimes prayed like the reverend at the church. Sometimes he just told them to "get with it" and believe in God, but most of the time he was good to them, and cared a lot about them—and he did too.

(Matthew 9:1-8)

One time a gang of people came to see Jesus. The place was full up, even the doors were full. While Jesus was talking real cool like, some other guys brought a sick guy on a bed. The sick guy was so jammed up he couldn't walk or anything. His friends couldn't get him in the door so they chopped a hole in the roof, tied some rope on it, and let it down to Jesus—very easy like. Jesus says, "Well, how about that? These guys sure got lots of faith—guess I'll help them out, man." So Jesus says, "OK, Baby, your sins is all forgot about."

But the sick guy don't get with that and some of the wheels in the crowd gets the idea that it just ain't right for Jesus to say that. So everybody is mixed up but mostly the sick guy. So Jesus figured guess I better really prove this to them, so he says to the sick guy "Stand up, man!" And he did. Then Jesus says, "Walk, man!" And he did. Then Jesus says, "You can hit the streets now, and take your bed." And he did too. The sick guy ain't sick no more and was real happy, so he's saying all kinds of good things about Jesus and saying thanks to God 'cause he can walk now.

The people who saw this was all shook up about it. Some says man, ain't that great. Some says that's real cool, like but anyway now they is getting the idea who Jesus is.

A Girl Who Was Sick

The Daughter of Jairus (Mark 5:22-43)

One of the big men of the church had a name like Jairus. He used to hear Jesus preach on the street like the Salvation Army and he seen some of those great things Jesus did like getting sick people better. Jairus had a girl who was sick and almost dead. Jairus was all shook up inside about it. So he goes to see Jesus. He says, "How about you takin' over and fixing up this kid of mine? Maybe you could just touch her and that would do it. It won't take much of you time, man." Jesus sees that the cat Jairus is all shook up about his kid and feels for him so he gets near him. The people says something real super may happen so they follows along. There was a real poor woman who was in a bad way—even the welfare lady didn't do much to help her 'cause she couldn't anyway. She thinks, "Jesus is supposed to help people, maybe he will help me." She's got it figured, "If I just touch him, it might do it." She had a rough time getting through the crowd, but she says, "If I just touch him I'll get well. So she touch him, and she did! Jesus says, "All right—

who did it?" (He knew all the time she did). So the woman says, so everyone can hear it, "I did it 'cause I was sick, man, and now I'm OK!" Jesus says that's right—it's 'cause she got lots of faith.

Then somebody comes and says, "Hey, Jairus, while you guys was messing around your kid died. You're too late to do any good now." Jesus says, "Cool it, Jairus. It's gonna be OK, you'll see." So when they gets to Jairus' house people was cryin' and yellin'. But Jesus is real cool and takes a few people and goes in the dead girl's room and says "I'm telling you to get up!" He said it like he means it—and he did too! And she did, she walked and was OK. Everybody got all shook up again and who wouldn't to see something like that. Then Jesus tells them to feed her, so she eats. So Jairus and his family goes the Jesus way after that. Be kinda funny if they didn't.

The Guy at the Pond
The Waters of Bethesda (John 5:1-6)

There was this pond that had a house built on the top of it like a dockhouse. The house had five porches and was a real crash pad. There was something screwy about this pond 'cause it got lots of bubbles in it. Some of the cats thought it was a heaven cat in the pond and if they got in the pond first they could get their sickness fixed

GOD IS BEAUTIFUL, MAN

up. So lots of people came there who got all kinds of trouble. Everyone figures he is gonna be first in.

One Sunday Jesus was out taking a walk to kill time. He sees a guy who has been sick for thirty-eight years. He had been there for a long time, everybody beating him out so he never made it.

Jesus takes pity on him. He says, "All right, you—pick up your bed and walk, man!" The man first thinks this guy's freaking out or something. But a funny thing happened and he got better—so he takes his bed, and would you believe he walked, and took his bed to his pad.

One of the lawyers who saw it starts bitchin 'cause the guy is carrying his bed on Sunday. He says, "Who gave you the word to do that?" He says, "I don't know." He was too happy to pay him attention anyway. A little while later the sick guy who got better sees Jesus in the church. He's pretty friendly to Jesus and he says to the lawyer, "There he is, that's my man." So the other lawyers started to chew him out 'cause he done work on Sunday. So Jesus tells them off, but good. And they still don't wise up to who he is. The wheels was all ready to bug Jesus. They was trying to get him and frame him. So they watched him all the time. They got mad when he fixed up a guy in a church one Sunday. Well, Jesus is getting fed up on this and figures it's time to have heart and face it. So he says, "What's the matter with you guys? What you want me to do? I think it's a good thing to help a guy even on Sunday. You want me beat on him or something? I suppose if he fell in the river you would let him drown if it was Sunday huh!" But they didn't pay no attention to him. So Jesus figures he'll trap them now. "If you cats had a pet dog and he fell in a hole like the sewer guys dig on Sunday—I bet you would pull him out. Right?" They didn't say nothing but they got the message all right.

The Funeral

The Son Who Was Dead (Luke 7:11-17)

Once Jesus went to another city. A whole bunch of people followed him, just to see what he was going to do next, and man was something in the works this time. The city had a main drag, and a market place. Guys used to hang around on the corners and talk all day. A lady had a son whose father was dead. The son conked out too. They had him in the house and everybody came to cry and feel sad, and have a few drinks.

Then they had a funeral, first some women crying then the body in the box. Some of his friends carried the casket. Everybody was broke up. Jesus and his people saw what was up and felt sorry for them, so he says, "Let's fix 'em up." So he goes over and touches the kid in the casket and the kid gets up. Jesus gives him back to his mother who was pretty surprised.

GOD IS BEAUTIFUL, MAN

Who Is This Guy?

Jesus Calms the Sea (Mark 4:37-41)

When the winds blow the lake gets rough with waves and the winds blow. It's pretty wild. One night Jesus wanted to go to the other side so he got in a rowboat. He was bushed so he got some shut-eye while they was rowing. Then it happened. A big blow came up, big waves and stuff. They all got scared except Jesus—he was asleep. They woke him up. "You better do something about this," they says, or we is done. So Jesus looks at the waves and says, "All right, knock it off." And would you believe they did. Then Jesus says, "What's the matter with you guys? Don't you got no faith?" Then they is starting to get wised and says, "Who is this guy? Even the waves do what he says."

Fishin'

The Lowering of the Nets (Matthew 4:18-22)

One day Jesus was out talkin' to some people by a lake. Then another big mob of people come along and started crowdin' and pushin', makin' a mess of things and they almost pushed him right in the lake. Not very far away there was a bunch of guys who was fishermen and they was cleanin' and washin' their nets and they had some boats too. So Jesus sees that they ain't usin' their boats even though one of them was sittin' in it so Jesus says, "Man, these guys is gonna push me out in the lake. How's about me usin' your boat?" So the guy that owned the boat, his name was Peter, said, "OK." So he pushed the boat out and he sat down in it and then he started talkin' to that mob. And they couldn't push him around and they could all see him.

Now Jesus wants to do somethin' to say thanks to Peter for letting him use the boat. Jesus knows the cats have been out fishin' all night and they ain't caught nothin'. So he figures he'll give 'em a little lift and he says to Peter, "OK, you guys put the net down on that side of the boat." Well Peter says, "Aw, come off it. We been fishin' all night and we ain't caught nothin'. Whatta you want us to do?" Well he didn't feel like foolin' around with it so he thinks he will just show him and so he put the net down and bingo the nets is full of fish. So Peter and his brother James say, "Hey, what gives here?" And they started pullin' in the nets like crazy and pretty soon the boats was so full that they started to sink. Well Peter feels pretty bad about this and how he acted so he says to Jesus, "How come you always help me? I ain't worth that much." But Jesus always cared about people so he said, "Well, OK, don't be scared from now on. And instead of catchin' fish I want you to help me kinda get ahold of other guys and help them to be what they oughta be."

Now this business of catchin' all them fish

GOD IS BEAUTIFUL, MAN

when they didn't think they was any around there made Peter and his brother Andrew and his other brother James and brother John decide that there must be somethin' to this guy Jesus so they decided to give up the fishin' bit and follow along with him.

Nutty Things
The Hidden Treasure (Matthew 13:44)

Jesus tells a story about a guy who was lookin' around in a old wrecked house and found a box in there that was full of bread. So he hid it again and then he went and he took everything he had—his automobile—and he hocked them. That was so he could get enough money to go back and buy the wrecked house. Then he would own the treasure box. He told it to make people understand that maybe getting a treasure like heaven, is worth givin' up all kinds of nutty things that you have in this world.

A Real Young Bread Man
Jesus and the Rich Man (Matthew 19:16-30)

One day all the people was havin' a great big picnic and Jesus and his guys was gettin' ready to go but Jesus wasn't quite ready. So he told his guys, "Go ahead over to the picnic." Now the big blast was bein' held in Jerusalem and when it was time for Jesus to take out after the place he had to go through a state named Samaria. Now the cats in one of the villages weren't too polite and they didn't want nobody, including Jesus, comin' in there to bug them. Now this gets James and John really teed off and they had a pretty low boiling point anyway. So they says to Jesus, "Shall we belt 'em around a bit?" Now Jesus don't go for that stuff so he says, "Naw, leave 'em alone. They ain't worth it anyway and besides I'm tryin' to help 'em." And he really didn't want to rough 'em up. So they went through another village. Now while they were goin' to another village a big crowd of people started followin' along. And on the way they was lots of muggers. On account of they was so many muggers they built big walls around the city and they had gates in the walls. One of these gates was so small they called it the eye of a needle.

Now as Jesus was movin' toward the big city there was a real young bread man who was a big wheel of some kind. Now this bread man runs up and he falls down on his knees in front of Jesus and he says, "OK, master, what kinda good things have I gotta do to live forever?" And Jesus says, "All you gotta do is the right things and just do what God wants you to do and get with them commandments." So the bread man says, "Which commandments, you got nine." So Jesus tells him a couple of the commandments and the guy says,

GOD IS BEAUTIFUL, MAN

"Oh, I already do that stuff. What else have I gotta do?" Then Jesus puts the clincher on him. He says, "Why don't you get all of your bread and give it to the poor people then come be one of my guys." Well that kinda stuff is no go for the bread man and he gets all busted up because he can't have his own way, and he leaves. So Jesus says, "These guys that've got themselves all jammed up with money find it hard to give a care, even about the kingdom of God." Then he says, "You see that little tiny gate up there? It would be easier for that great big camel to go through there than for the bread man to give a care about God."

Then there was another rich man. His name was Zach and he lived in a city called Jericho. He was a big shot tax collector. Now lots of people in Jericho had heard about Jesus and when they heard he was comin' they all came out to give a look at him. It was such a big gang of people that maybe even the cops put up them planks to keep the people on the sidewalk. And this guy Zach was just a little guy and he couldn't see over the crowd so he climbed up a tree.

When Jesus came near the tree a real wild thing happened. He looks up and he sees Zach and he said, "Hey, Zach, I'm gonna stay at your pad tonight." Well this made Zach real high and he beats it down out of that tree and takes him home. Well the crowd don't study no tax collector and they said, "What's the matter with this guy

Jesus. How come he is goin' to that guy's home? He ain't no good." And they got very put out about it.

Now while they was in the pad, Zach tries to give Jesus a little bit of a con job and he said, "You know, I'd give half of all my stuff to the poor people and if I over charge anybody I give it back to them double, twice." Now this gets Jesus real happy and he said, "You really do believe don't you, and you do try to do what God wants you to do. That's great, Zach, I like that and God's really with you."

Watch Out, You Jokers and Hipes
The Scribes and Pharisees (Matthew 23:13-23)

Watch out, you bunch of jokers, you bunch of hipes, you turn everybody off and you even turn yourself off, and you get it fixed up so nobody can go in. You're gonna get it, you bunch of jerks. You go trackin' all over the blocks, just to sign up one guy and when he gets signed up you get him in more hell than you are in yourself. You stupid nuts! You say that if someone promises to God it don't mean nothin' but if he shakes hands with you he's gotta stick by you. What's the matter with you guys? Don't you think God counts for something? You're so blind you're gettin' everything all bawled up about which is the most important things. You get all shook up if you don't

GOD IS BEAUTIFUL, MAN

have the most hep clothes or shoes or beads. Don't you know treatin' a guy like he's something and showin' him that you really care about him is more important than all the words you could ever speak and all the things you ever got.

Five Stupid, Five Hep
The Ten Virgins (Matthew 25:1-13)

One time after Jesus left the church he started tellin' his people about how the city was gonna get wrecked up and how he would come some day again. And when he did, he was gonna be the judge and that only God knew when he was gonna come again but that they'd better be ready or else.

So he told 'em a story about ten gals that never got married but who were always helpin' out at other weddings. Five of them were pretty stupid and the other five were pretty hep. The stupid ones took their flashlights but they didn't put any batteries in 'em and the hep ones put the batteries in. They had to have them because the guy that was gettin' married was comin' at night and the lights weren't working in the high rises.

Now while they was waiting all these unmarried gals went to sleep. Then when they was asleep somebody started yellin', "Here he comes, the guy that's gonna get married." Then all those gals tried to put their flashlights on but the stupid ones' lights wouldn't go on so they said to the hep ones, "Hey, give us some of your batteries." But the hep ones knew if they took their batteries out then their lights wouldn't go on. So they said, "Why don't you go down to the drugstore and buy your own?" So they ran down to the drugstore and while they were down there, the guy that was getting married came. So that meant that only the hep gals got to go into the big feast and party blast. While they was in there the stupid ones came and they started bangin' on the door and makin' a big racket and demonstrating about not being let in. But the guy that was in charge of the blast wouldn't let them in 'cause they hadn't got ready when they was supposed to.

Jesus told this story so everybody would know they supposed to get things figured out right now then they'll be ready.

Spooks—Get Out!
Casting out Evil Spirits (Mark 1:23-26)

One Sunday a bunch of guys who didn't believe that Jesus cared about sick people and made them get well, started shootin' off their mouths about him. Sayin' all kinds of dirty things, mostly that he didn't have nothin' to do with God, and he was really a very bad character and that he got his power from some kinda witch or something. But Jesus knows what they're thinkin' about. So instead of blowin' his top he gets these guys together to kind of cool it off a bit. So he says, "How can the devil or a witch or something like that be around me?" Then he says, "How can you be God's man and belong to the devil at the same time?" Well they knows that can't be. So then Jesus decides, I guess I'll just have to show these guys.

Then there was a lot of guys that came over to see Jesus who lived up near the cemetery. Everybody was scared of them. Fact nobody even dared to walk on the same side of the street that they lived on. Some people tried to tie them up but they only busted the rope up. One of them was real wild and he came runnin' after Jesus and Jesus tells the evil spirit to get out of this guy. Well, the evil spirits did and they went and jumped in a bunch of pigs and the pigs gets all mixed up about it and they runs down a big hill into a pond and they gets drowned. Well now the pig keepers don't go for that and they ran into the city and told people what happened and then the people in the city came out to see what's goin' on. But, boy, were they ever surprised. For they saw the wild guy that they knew and he was OK. He even had clothes on and he was talkin' good. Now this gets the people all bugged up and they ask Jesus to get out of there and Jesus left but as he was goin' the man who got straightened out asked if he could go with him. But Jesus says, "No, you can help better if you go back to your own people and tell them what God did for you." And he did.

How About That?

Walking on the Water (Mark 6:45-52)

One night Jesus was off all by himself talkin' to God and prayin' and thinkin' things. He was out by the lake and the wind was blowin' like hell and the waves was bustin' over the breakwater and the moon was out. Jesus looks out on the lake and sees the boat full of the guys he likes the best and man were they ever in trouble! The waves was beltin' 'em around and they couldn't make things go with the oars and it looked like they was goin' to get swamped and drowned. But Jesus is a nice guy so he decides to go help 'em, and holy cripes he walks right on the water. Now the guys in the boat looked up and they see Jesus comin' walkin' on the water and this gets 'em even more scared. One of them says, "Yeow, it's a ghost!" So Jesus sees they're scared and he said, "Aw, don't be scared, it's only me." Well Peter gets pretty high about this and jumps right out of the boat to go and meet Jesus walkin' on the water. And Jesus says, "Good for you, man, come on over." So Peter tried it but then he spies those big waves and the water and he starts to sink. So Peter lets go with a big bellow, "Help!" Then Jesus grabs him by the hand and throws him back in the boat and he was safe again. Then Jesus helps them get back to the shore all safe and the guys say, "How about that, he is even the boss over the waters," and that made them believe even more who Jesus was.

GOD IS BEAUTIFUL, MAN

The Loan Sharks

The Story of the Money Changers (Mark 11:15-19)

One time Jesus decides he is going to go up to the church. Back in them days they had kind of a wierdo way of doing things in churches. They used to stick sheep or oxen or pigeons. And on account of people had to come a long ways sometimes it was easier to buy one of them there things and then take it into church and stick it. They called it a sacrifice. They was some guys like loan sharks, gyp artists who set up stores near the church and started sellin' sheep and ox and pigeons and double charging people 'cause they knew they couldn't get 'em any place else. Then they was some other kind of people. They called 'em money changers. On account of people had to come from other places and their money was no good where they were. Then it got all the more mixed up because the church had its own money. So the people had to take the regular money and turn it in and get the church money back 'fore they could put it in the basket. And the guys that used to change the money like the loan sharks charged you an awful lot for doin' it. And the Revs. in the church got cut in on it too.

Well, this day Jesus comes and he sees what's goin' on and it don't look like a church at all but it looks more like a vegetable market down on the corner with stuff all over the sidewalk and most people was interested in sellin' stuff rather than goin' to church. Well this gets Jesus really teed off and he got ahold of a whip. Then he takes the whip and he yells, "All right, you bunch of jerks, get outta here." Then he tipped over the tables and he yells, "You're makin' my Father's house like a store." Well, these guys gets real scared and they see that Jesus really means it and that he's groovin' up and down in front of them so they don't do nothin' 'bout it. So then one guy says, "Hey man, what right have you got to do these things?" Then Jesus tells 'em, "You kill me and in three days I'll be right back here again." But they didn't understand this. Well, anyway, he shook people up so that they really began to believe that he was right when he said he was the Son of God. Then the people began to pay attention to him and follow 'im and even some of the Revs. did it too.

A Tree in the Park
The Unfruitful Tree (Luke 13:6-9)

Jesus was tryin' to help people get on the ball, hopin' that they'd get it. The park guys came down the street and they planted a tree. And the next year it didn't have no leaves and it didn't grow and it didn't do nothin'. So they cut it up and they said, "It ain't no good, that's why we got rid of it." And if a guy isn't good for nothin' then he is just like a dead tree.

GOD IS BEAUTIFUL, MAN

Then Jesus tells 'em that sometimes the tree don't grow too fast 'cause there's too much cement around and it don't get enough water. And how sometimes people who live in the houses come out and put water around the tree, but if they don't, then you cut it down. And all Jesus was tryin' to tell them was, better make sure if you're gonna do anything you're gonna have time to do it.

The Panhandler

The Blind Beggar (Luke 18:35-43)

One Sunday morning Jesus was with these guys and he saw a beggar like the kind you see hawkin' pencils or a panhandler tryin' to get a dime or a quarter or something. Well, Jesus did the craziest thing you ever heard. He took some clay from the road and he spit on it . . . yeck! Then he mixed it all up and he puts it on the blind guy's eyes. Then he tells him to go wash it off. Well maybe the blind guy didn't want that sticky stuff all over him so he went and he washed it off and then he went home. Well, the guys in the next apartment hardly knew him he was so different. And some didn't even believe it was him. They thought he was a fake of some kind. So then they began buggin' him how this came about and how he got cured and how he got his sight back again. Now the people that lived in that apartment house didn't believe in Jesus much anyway and they didn't want him to get the credit for gettin' the man fixed up. Finally they brought the man before the big bosses who didn't like Jesus very much either. So they began askin' him all kinds of questions about how he got healed up. Then they began sayin' on account of he did things on Sunday that he wasn't supposed to do that he couldn't be God's man. But they couldn't make him change his mind when he told them Jesus fixed him up, so they threw him out.

Jesus heard that they cast the man out so he went lookin' for the guy and he said to him, "You believe in God?" and the man answered, "Sure." And Jesus said, "You believe in me?" and the guy says, "Sure I do." Jesus answered, "OK, when you see me you see God." And the man said, "Yep, I knew it." And he believed.

Thanks, Man

Healing the Lepers (Luke 17:11-19)

Once there was ten guys who had a very bad sickness. Nobody could get near 'em, so they spies Jesus and they says, "Hey, man, how 'bout cooling it with us?" They knew that Jesus always gave a care about people who were sick and was getting pushed around by other people so they figured they had nothin' to lose if they asked him to help them. Now when Jesus hears them he feels

GOD IS BEAUTIFUL, MAN

real sorry for them so he tells them to go show themselves to the priest. And they did. But on the way they got all fixed up and they didn't have that leprosy any more.

Now you would think these cats would feel pretty good about that and at least stop by to say thanks, but they didn't. Only one guy when he found out he was OK again even bothered to yell back thanks. He went and he knelt down in front of Jesus and he said, "Thanks, man". Well, Jesus sees this and he said, "Hey, I thought there was ten guys that got cured. Where are the others?" Then Jesus says to the other guy, "OK, you can get up and go on your way. It wasn't so much me that fixed you up as that you really believed".

Settling a Mess
Jesus and Little Children (Mark 10)

The guys that was always around Jesus used to have a lot of gummin' goin' on about who's the big man. Just like when you fight with your brother or your sister. Jesus gets fed up with this so one day he says, "You guys, set down. I'm gonna settle this right now." This kinda shakes them up a little so they sits down. Then Jesus says, "Now what are you guys fightin' about this time?" Well, they didn't say nothin'. They just looks down at the ground or maybe made like they didn't hear or that they didn't know what was goin' on, but they did. Then one yaks off and says, "Who's gonna be the big guy in heaven?" Well, Jesus figures this is comin' and he's ready for 'em so he just says, "Well if you wanna be first, you gotta be last. And if you wanna be the wheel you gotta be the errand boy." Then one of them says, "Why, what kinda stuff is that. Whatta you talkin' about? You playin' games or something?" But all he really meant was, if you really wanta be somebody you gotta treat people like they was somebody.

These guys always figured that Jesus was going to be a big king and all they really wanted was to be pals with him. And to be next to him.

Well Jesus figures that they ain't gettin what he's sayin' and he sees a real little cat playin' in a sandbox and he called the little cat and says, "Come on over here, sonny." And the cat did and Jesus picked him up and sat him on his knees and held him and then he looked at the disciples real straight like and he said, "You gotta be like one of these if you want to get anywhere." Well now Jesus' people are beginnin' to swing with it and they gettin' the idea about how little kids really loves other people and other people really loves them and that it's easy to do nice things for little kids and that maybe they better start thinkin' about helpin' older people too. And that when you do nice things for other people you are pretty big, real big like. And it don't really make no difference if you're one or two. 'Cause with God you're always number one.

A Cool Wedding
The Wedding at Cana (John 2:1-11)

Everybody likes a cool story and this is about a wedding and that's about as cool as you can get —most of the time, that is. One day Jesus' mother says, "Jesus, how 'bout you and me and all those guys that are always hangin' around with you, goin' over to the weddin'? They're having a big blast after they get through at the church, and everybody's going." So Jesus said, "OK, so we'll go too".

The weddin' blast is over at the labor union hall and they got the room all fixed up pretty. They gotta combo and chairs all over the place and lotsa food and drinks. Well the big drink at this blast is wine. And everybody is guzzlin' more than his share, so they runs out of the stuff and probably by this time all the liquor stores is closed and there's no place to get some more, except bootleg stuff.

Now Jesus' mother feels sorry for the people puttin' on the blast and she says to Jesus, "Now ain't that too bad, they got no more wine." Now Mary's kinda pushin' Jesus a little bit to do one of those things called miracles, which is kind of spooky. And Jesus ain't so big on lettin' the word get out that he can do them miracle things. But after all, it's his mother that's askin' him. And anyway she figured on account of he liked everybody he'd do somethin' to make sure they got enough wine to go around. So Jesus turns to the waiters and tells 'em, "You see those big pots out there, fill 'em up with water." So they fill 'em up with water and Jesus says, "OK, you guys, let the guy puttin' on the blast try some." And he did and man, was he ever shook up. He turned and he said, "You know most people put out the best stuff first, but this is the best stuff I ever tasted. Where did you get it?" But the ruler, he was just as surprised as anybody else, and nobody still knows how Jesus turned that water into wine. And that's the first time he ever did one of those spooky miracle things, but it was a pretty good start.

A Creep Makes It

Nicodemus (John 3:1-15)

One night Jesus met a guy named Nicodemus. How's that for a handle? He was a real wheel in the government. During the day people was always buggin' him so the only time he got to talk to Jesus was at night when nobody else was around. Or maybe it was because he was scared to have people see him with Jesus 'cause lots of people thought that Jesus was a kook. Anyway, they got together.

Now this guy Nicodemus knew that Jesus had his thing goin' for him but he wasn't sure what the thing was but that Jesus sure enough must be tuned in with God. So Nicodemus says, "Man, we

GOD IS BEAUTIFUL, MAN

know you're swingin' with God or you couldn't do these way out things you're doin'." So Jesus says to him, "Well you better swing with God too if you want to do God's thing and get to see God some day." So this guy Nick, he says, "How could I do that, I'm gettin' kind of old and it's gettin' kind of rough to get into a new groove, man." So Jesus says, "Oh, no, it ain't. You got born once didn't you, and you didn't have to do much about it. You was just a little baby, and now look, you're a big man with lots of bread. So it's like gettin' born again and startin' all over. By believin' in yourself that you are somebody and believin' in God that he thinks that you are somebody too. But you gotta start out believin' in something." So Jesus tells Nick how it was when Moses was helpin' people get outa Egypt and them snakes came and about how those that believed in God got through alright. Then Jesus tells Nick how some hoods is gonna put him on a cross and get rid of him. Then Jesus tells Nick how God loves everybody no matter how low down they was even if they was winos or a drug freak or cons or guys with a lotta bread. And more than that he said they was gonna live forever. And we know that's right 'cause Jesus was God's Son. Then Jesus tells Nicodemus that 'cause he was God's Son, God sent him here. But he didn't come to blast people out and tell 'em off, or get mad or yell at 'em but to help 'em but mostly to help 'em have faith in God and in themselves and if they did that and if they really believed it they could really get pulled out of the mess that they is in now.

Like, Great, Man
The Samaritan Woman (John 4:4-12)

One day Jesus and his people were walkin' from one city to the other and it was a lot of blocks away and it was kinda hot and they was pretty thirsty. And they were lookin' for a place to get a drink. They found a drinkin' place and all got a drink then Jesus sat down to get a good rest. And his people went into the city to get somethin' to eat.

While Jesus was restin' his poor feet a broad came along to get some water. And of all the screwy things, she put it in the jar that she carried on the top of her head. Now Jesus is still thirsty so he says, "Hey, gal, how's about givin' me a drink of water?" Well this kinda shakes the gal up 'cause she can tell from the way his clothes looks that he's from another part of the city and she ain't friends with nobody from that part of the city. And she knows too that them people don't even speak to people like her.

But Jesus, he's real cool like so he says, "It's all right, girl, I ain't gonna hurt you. But you know somethin', if you knew who I was and what I could do for you I kinda think you'd be askin' me for somethin' like a drink of water."

GOD IS BEAUTIFUL, MAN

Well, the broad don't get with that so she says, "You know, man, that water is a long way down there and I got nothin' to pull it up with." Then she says to herself, "Wonder who this guy is." So she says to Jesus, "You some kind of big shot or somethin'?" Then Jesus, still bein' real cool like said, "You know, after you drink that water, you're gonna get thirsty again but what I got in mind to give you means you're never goin' to lose it, and it'll stick with you forever."

Now Jesus never turned anybody off and he knew that lots of people didn't think very much of this woman but this guy Jesus he is just as interested in her as he was in that rich cat Nicodemus. But this woman she's not too bright and she figures that Jesus is tryin' to give her some kind of magic water or a con job so she says, "OK, I'll take some of that water, then I'll never get thirsty again and I'll never have to come back to this place again." But Jesus ain't thinkin' about that kinda water. He's thinkin' of that kind of stuff that makes you feel real good inside.

So Jesus says, "I guess I better level with this gal." And he tells her that he knows all about her and he knows that she's got a pretty bad record and all the times she got married and divorced and it wasn't always the husband's fault. Well this kinda shook her up but good! She says, "Well I know there's supposed to be a guy come along who is supposed to make everything easy for us to understand." Then she kinda gets the idea maybe this is him. And Jesus says, "I'm the guy."

Well this makes her pretty happy and she gets so spooked up about it that she ran into the city and forgot her jar of water and she gets a whole mob of people and she really gets them all worked up and they came out to see who this guy was. Then they listen to see what Jesus got to say and a lotta them sure got straightened out too. And it all started with that one broad who took time to listen.

Big Parade

The Palms (John 12)

There was a big Holy Day comin'. They called it the Passover. So Jesus and his people figured they ought to go to Jerusalem for the big blast. When the people hears about it they decided they ought to have a great big parade just to show him how much they really go for him. It's like when the cops set up the barricades and they have big bands and floats and all that kind of stuff. Except it wasn't quite like that. There was a great big crowd of people all along the streets. They didn't have time to put up all the flags and stuff like that but they wanted to do things up real good. They broke the branches off the trees when the parks department guys weren't lookin' and some of them even got their best coats to take with them for the big parade.

When they were gettin' near the city Jesus tells

his people to go into a little town and they would find a jackass and its baby which nobody had ever taken a ride on before. But he told them not to heist it but to tell the guy that owned it that the Lord needed it, which is pretty groovy too. And he gives it to them and they take it back to Jesus and one of them puts their coat on its back and Jesus sits on it. So now the parade's all set. And when Jesus and his people get to the city limits they all starts cheerin' on account of they didn't have any band. And they began wavin' the branches from the trees and puttin' them in the road and other people began puttin' their coats in the road so it wouldn't be dirty. Maybe that's because they didn't have street sweepers in those days. Some people started yellin' hallelujah. And others started yellin' hosanna and some others yelled God bless you, just like the preachers in the church do. But everybody began to make out like he was their king, and everybody was pretty happy about the whole thing and they figured it was a great day.

Don't Forget Me

The Last Supper (John 13:1-38)

Jesus had been doin' all kinds of groovy things like teachin' people how to make it with others. He had been fixin' people up that was sick and some that had gimpy legs and some that couldn't see. Then he told them a Holy Day was comin'. One of those days that the Catholic kids don't have to go to their school, sorta like that. Then after that he told them somethin' that sounded kinda scarey. That there was some guys that had a contract for him and that he was gonna get killed.

There was some cats and their boss was a guy named Caiaphas. They were the guys that had the contract and they were tryin' to fix up a program so that they could get him so that not too many people would get them too. And they thought if they could get everybody mad at him that that would do it. There was a guy in the sus gang. His name was Judas and he was a rat fin. So this dirty rat fink he says to the pres of the gang, Caiaphas, "What's in it for me if I put the finger on him?" So they figure they will give him thirty bucks which he grabbed. Then he figured out what would be the best time and that he would just play it nice and easy like until he got a good chance.

The Holy Day was what they called Passover. And they used to have a big feast like Thanksgiving or Christmas or something like that. So they finds a room like in a boarding house that was on the second floor. They get around this big table which had all kinds of food on it. Now while they was eating everybody was gassin' and they got into a stupid fight over which one is the biggest wheel. Now Jesus don't go for this. So instead of bawlin' 'em out he did a real groovy thing. He took a towel then he dumped some water into a bowl and he started to wash the feet of those guys and then wipe them off with the towel. Now them cats get with that pretty quick because they know that he's the boss and look what he's doin'. So then they didn't have any more fights over who is the biggest wheel.

Now that dirty rat fink Judas was there too. Jesus must have known about it and what the fink was gonna do because while they was sittin' at the table Jesus says, "One of you guys is gonna turn me in." And then they all looked at each other and they was pretty shook by that. Then they all said, "Who's gonna do it? Is it me?" So when they said, "Who is it?" Jesus says, "It's the one that I'm passin' the food to. And he starts to hand it over to Judas and Judas says, "Is it me?" And Jesus says, "You said it, man." And then the rat fink takes the food anyway. So Jesus said, "Why don't we hurry up and get this over with."

Things was gettin' real serious now and that's when Jesus started that thing that the preachers call the Communion. Sometimes they call it the Lord's Supper. Jesus picked up a piece of bread and he busted it and then he prayed and then he gave it to his disciples and he said, "Eat it and it'll make you think of me." Then he took a cup and it was filled with wine and again he prayed. Then he gave it to them and told them to "Drink up and it'll make you think of my blood which is gonna get spilt all over the place for you." Then he told them every time you do this think of me, and don't forget me either.

Then Jesus tells them not to get too shook up just 'cause he was goin' away. 'Cause he was goin' to get a place fixed up for them and he'd come and pick them up again. Then he told them a lotta real groovy things about he was really the real truth and his way was the way to really live and how they should do all the things that the Bible tells you to do. Then he said, "I'm like the trunk of a tree and you're like the branches that grow off it."

Then after they started prayin' again they began singin' and feelin' sorry about what was gonna happen and about that contract that got put on Jesus. And as they were goin' out Peter who still thinks he is the wheel starts blowin' off again. He said no matter what happened he was going to stick by him even if he got killed. Jesus don't like this and he said, "You're talkin' outta the side of your mouth again. Before the rooster crows three times you're gonna tell people you never saw me before." Well the big man don't believe this and he says, "I'm tellin' ya, I'll always stick by you." And the disciples they said the same thing.

But it didn't work out that way 'cause when that rat fink turned Jesus in he was all alone and there was no one there.

Don't Get Shook Up

In My Father's House (John 14:1-12)

Don't get all shook up. You said you believed in God, you gotta believe in Jesus too. God's got lots of places and that's for real too. And Jesus goes to fix one up for you. And when he gets it all fixed up he's comin' back to get you. Then we can both be there together. And Jesus said, "You know where I'm goin', man, and you know how to get there." Well, one of the guys called Thomas said, "How can we know the way?" Then Jesus, he ain't shook up at all, he just looks at him real nice like and says, "Oh, don't let that worry you. All you gotta do is follow me and I'll show you the way." Then he says somethin' else, "If you knew me like you ought to know me you'd know God too." Then another one of the Jesus' people says, "So OK if you show us, we'll believe it."

Well Jesus don't like this so much so he said, "Man, have I been around here all this time with you guys and you still don't know who I am? Don't you know that when you see me you see what God's like too. Don't you believe that God and I are real close with each other and that what I got to say to you is what God's got to say too. All you gotta believe is that we're together. And if you think some of the things that I've been doin' is real big, then you're gonna do even bigger things man."

After Jesus Busts out of the Grave
Jesus Appears (John 20:1—21:24)

Mary was in the graveyard and she was bawlin'
and she looked in the grave and she was bawlin'
pretty hard and she saw two guys with white
things on sittin' where they put the body of Jesus.
One was up near where the head was supposed to
be and the other near the feet. They looked up at
her and said, "What you bawlin' about?" She said,
"Somebody took him away and I don't know
where they put him." And she was so choked up
that she turned away and she saw Jesus standin'
there but she didn't even know who he was. So
he says, "What are you bawlin' about, who are
you lookin' for?" She thinks it's the grave digger
that's sayin' these things, and she said, "If you
took him away why don't you tell me where you
put him so I can go get him and bring him back."
Jesus is kinda touched by this so he says *very*
slow and easy, "Mary." Well Mary looks and then
she knows who it is and she reaches out to shake
his hand. Jesus says, "You better not touch me, I
haven't gone back up to Heaven yet, but I tell you
what I want you to do. You go in and tell my people that I'm OK and that I'm not dead and that
I'm goin' back to God." Well, she's pretty shook
up about this but she did it anyway.

Then one Sunday night the Jesus' people were
altogether in a rooming house and they locked the
door because they were scared of everybody. And

Jesus came and stood right in the middle and he said, "Peace." Then he said, "Take a look at my hands." And they did. Then he said, "Look where that soldier stuck me." And they did. That made them believe who he really was. But one of them, didn't really believe, because he wasn't there when it happened. When the Jesus people told him about it he said, "Yeah, yeah, so what else is new? Who do you think you're kiddin'? I got to touch him before I believe it."

A little later they were back in the same place and this guy Thomas is with them, and Jesus came again. He said, "So OK men, you don't wanna believe? Put your finger here in my hands and put it on my side, then cut out your kiddin' and start believin'." Then he said, "OK, you believe only because you see, but a guy who believes without seein' me is better off than you are."

Saul Gets Turned Around
Saul's Conversion (Acts 9:1-9)

Once there was a guy named Saul who was a pretty mean guy and he didn't want nothin' to do with the Jesus' people except to beat 'em up and throw 'em in the can.

Once he was ridin' along the road and there was a big light came in the sky and it scared the hell out of him and he fell down on the ground. Then he heard a voice saying, "Saul, what are you mockin' me out for?" So then this guy Saul didn't see nobody so he says, "Who's that talkin' like that?" And he hears the voice saying, "I'm Jesus, the guy you're mockin' out." And then the Jesus voice says, "Get up off the ground there, man, and go on into that city then we'll tell you what to do."

Now there are lots of guys traveling with Saul and they are hearin' the voice but they don't see nothin' and they think it's kinda spooky. So Saul gets up and opened up his eyes and he was blind. Then the guys that was with him give him one of them white canes with the red thing on it and took him into the city. Then they found a room for him and put him up in the boardin' house. And he stayed there for three days and didn't have nothin' to eat and didn't have nothin' to drink and he was very lonely.

Now there was another guy in that city and he had a funny name, Ananias. He had a dream and thought he heard a voice say get ready and go over on Sycamore Street in the boardin' house and ask for a man named Saul. Now this gets even more groovy 'cause all the time this was goin' on Saul's havin' a dream and in the dream he sees the guy named Ananias come and puttin' his hands on him like the preach down at the revival camp does and then he could see again.

Well, Ananias is thinkin' about this and he remembers he's been hearin' about this guy and that this guy Saul's been puttin' the finger on all

GOD IS BEAUTIFUL, MAN

the Jesus people and he don't want nothin' to do with him. Then Ananias hears this voice sayin', "Never mind all that stuff. You just go and put your hands on him like I told you to do and I'll take care of him." So Ananias goes over to Sycamore Street and finds this guy Saul. When he sees him he don't know what he was afraid about because the guy can't see, so he just walks up real big like and he says, "Brother Saul, I'm here so that you can see again." And he touched him like he was supposed to do and some things that look like those funny things on fishes fell off his eyes and man, was he ever glad about that! So he stood up and Ananias gave him somethin' to eat and in a little while he was strong again. And that fixed him up in another way too. 'Cause he got to be one of the Jesus people.

Getting Sins Fixed Up
(Acts 10:34)

One day there was a guy named Peter in a revival tent on a empty lot and he started preachin' at the people. So he says, "I know that God treats everybody just like they was somebody and if you live right and if you're square it don't make no difference who you are or what you are. And if you think about it you remember how Jesus got born and got baptized in the water and how God poured something holy on him and everywhere he went people liked him and he did those miracle things and how he always helped everybody, especially those that got spooked up by the devil. Well I know you know it, but we seen it happen. We even saw them kill him by puttin' him on a cross and bangin' in the nails and we even seen him after he busted out of the grave. And we ate and had somethin' to drink with him, and that's why we listened when he told us to start preachin' and tellin' all you guys and cats that everyone that believes will get his sins all fixed up."

Tell 'Em Off

(Acts 28:26)

God says, "Go and tell these people off. Tell 'em they listened but they didn't really hear and they didn't know what was goin' on. Tell 'em to look but they didn't see nothin', mostly because they're stupid. Your ears is plugged up, maybe with the things like you wear in swimmin' and they got their eyes closed and if they didn't do these things they'd hear and see what God want's them to see and then they'd understand. Then if they did I'd fix them up."

Paul Writes to the Cats in Rome

(Letter to the Romans)

Dear Romans:

This letter is for all of you that are on God's side. Every place I go I hear about you guys. Peo-

GOD IS BEAUTIFUL, MAN

ple always talkin' how you're so loyal to God. So that makes me think of you every time I get around to doin' my prayin'. And I'm prayin' that I can get back and see you again, mostly because I wanta do some more preachin'.

I'm not all shook up about the gospel, even if people poke fun at me 'cause I believe it. That's because it's God's way of getting everybody pulled out of the mess they're in, if they believe it to. And it don't make no difference who you are.

Everything always turns out OK if you love God and you do what you know he wants you to do, and if God is on our side, what you worrying about, man? Don't you know that nothin' can change that, even if you're poor, like you don't have the best clothes or if other guys are climbing up on you, you more than win when everything goes wrong because God loves you. Don't you really believe then when you're really down that nothin' can break God away from you. Once you dig that you are really in.

Now on account that God's gonna stick by you, I think you better stick by him and that's the best way you can tell him how much you love him. Don't be dragged down by the guys that call you chicken if you don't do somethin' nutty like they want you to. Have heart and show them what's the right way by what you do.

Then there's another thing I better tell you. And that's not to get too high about yourself. But don't get too low either. Because you are worth somethin'. We are all a little different you know. It's like this, man, one guy can sing pretty good, another guy can do pretty good in school work, another guy is pretty good at making models, another guy's pretty good at helpin' you think straight, so we all better pitch in and help each other. When we do that it means there is some real love. It's easy to get tired of that kind of jazz, so you better learn to be cool with the other guy, if he gives up too quick.

One more thing, don't get mad too quick. Maybe the guy who is blasting you out has got his own bag of troubles and it may help him a little bit if he takes it out on you. And when another guy is real happy you'll feel great if you are happy with him. Don't forget too that nobody's so low down that you should check him off and don't get too big for your own thinking either. If anybody gets hungry why don't you give him a bite of your hot dog and if he is thirsty maybe you could share your pop with him. Don't let yourself get boxed in by bad things. And when you are thinkin' about others and tryin' to help them it's pretty hard to get a box around you.

Listen, Brother

Life as a Christian (Romans 12)

Listen, brother, you gotta good deal from God so how 'bout you payin' him back with another good one. Instead of throwin' a penny or a nickel

GOD IS BEAUTIFUL, MAN

at the Salvation Army why don't you let God use you. 'Cause when you do that's the best thing you can do. Don't be afraid to be called chicken 'cause you scared 'bout what other people gonna say about you. But let God make you over and maybe even fix up your brains. Then you'll really know what a great thing really is and how it's supposed to be.

Don't think you're such a big man, but only take a good look at yourself. And when you get to thinkin' you're so big, maybe you can think about your hands and your feet and your eyes and your ears and how none of them would be no good if you didn't have the other things. Everybody's got somethin' they can do real good and that's what we really ought to do. If you can talk real good like you better talk about God, and if you're pretty good at showing another kid how to fix something and do something then you better do it. And if you're pretty good at helping another guy up when he's down, then you better do that. And it's a pretty good thing to do it 'cause you want to do it and because it helps somebody and when you do it—smile. Love has got to be for real. Get away from bad things and hold on to good things. Treat everybody like they really was somebody. Do all your work and don't be a lazy bum. Get hep to what God wants you to do and when things don't go right, don't give up too quickly. If you've got more food and more stuff than somebody else, give 'em a break and give 'em a little bit of the stuff that you got.

When somebody's down on you, don't cuss 'em out and chew 'em out. Ask God to bless 'em. Be happy with those that are happy and when somebody's down in the dumps, go down with 'em. Don't be a big head and don't think you're so smart either. And if someone gives you a dirty deal don't pay 'em back with a dirty deal, even if you want to. Never try to get even with somebody. Remember God gets 'em and usually he does a better job than you do. Don't let bad things mess you up.

How to Treat Another Guy
(Romans 13:8-14)

Don't owe nobody nothin', except to like another guy and when you do that you won't have no trouble with the fuzz. You heard about God's laws, about no whorin' around or killin' anybody or swipin' their stuff. While there's another way of puttin' it, it's like this: If you love the guy that lives next door to you as much as yourself you won't have no trouble, 'cause you won't be able to do him no dirt. And when you really give a care about somebody else, then you're doin' what God wants you to do.

It's time you sharpened up about these things and get hep to what's goin' on. So let's knock off those bad things and stand up and fight like a man for the good things and act like you really was somebody. No more drunk parties and cussin' and sayin' dirty things or fightin' or gettin' sore because you don't have the things that other people has got. Because it's better to give a care about them and you don't know what troubles they got anyway.

Love Letter
The Way of Love (I Corinthians 13)

Dear Corinthians:

I wrote a letter to the Romans because they didn't dig the idea that everybody is different and all of us can do different things. And even though somebody maybe can do something better than you can doesn't mean you can't do something better than they can. That's cause God made us all different. But he is still the God of all of us.

Take a look at your own body. The hand's different from the eye and your foot is different from your knee and your ear is different from your nose, and that's a pretty good thing. God gave every one of those things a job to do and they better do it or you're done in for sure. The knee don't think it's more important than the foot and the ear don't think it's more important than the nose, but they all work together and that makes you. And that's how God wants everybody workin' together to make a better world for him.

Listen, you guys, if I came there blasting and sounding off and didn't do it because I really cared about you, all I'd be is a great big noise. And if I was the smartest guy in the world and I knew what was gonna happen tomorrow to you and if I had enough faith in God to tell the building to get outta the way and I didn't do it because I really cared about you then I'm a zero. And if I gave away everything I ever got and didn't do it because I cared about you, then it wouldn't make no difference at all.

Don't you know that the most important thing in the world is love? It's always kind and cool. It never gets shook up, it never sounds off. It never gets mad at people and nasty at them. It never tries to get its own way and it never feels good when things go wrong for the next guy. But it always feels good when things go right for him. Don't you know that love always sticks by a guy? That it's always got lots of hopes and it never, never gives up? Everything else will get done in someday. But love will always stick around. You remember when you were just a little cat, how you used to fight with your brothers and your sisters, and the only one you could ever think about was yourself? Well, now you are grown up and it's time to see yourself. And the most important things you can see in yourself are faith and hope and love, and the best of all is love because it never goes away. And that's about all I got to say to you, 'cause that's most important of all.

God's Gonna Stick by You

(Philippians)

Dear Phil:

Man, do I ever feel good every time I think about you, Phil. And every time I go up to the church I light a candle and say a prayer for you. I'm sure glad you're my friend right from the very beginning.

And another thing I am sure about, and that's God's always gonna stick by you.

Man, when the Lord's around you, you can always be glad and maybe even sing or yell some hallelujahs like the people down at the Tabernacle.

Let everybody know how cool you are and that you don't get shook up and bugged about anything and how you ask God for lots of different things and give him thanks when you light a candle and say a prayer. And like the hippies say, "Peace."

And before I sign off of this letter, Phil, stick with the things that are for real and good and fair and clean and slow and easy.

Then if you're good at something and if it's worth it, have real cool thoughts that don't get your insides all angried up and then you really will have that peace that the hippies talk about.

Real Strong Like

The Armor of God (Ephesians 6:10-20)

You better get real strong like so that you won't be a turkey. And then we can stand up against a tricky man. There's a real big rumble going on with those things that get inside you and bugs you and stirs you up, so you'd better take up God's part. Then you'll be ready when the rumble comes on your street and nobody will be able to push you around. Maybe you could look like them knight cats in the movies with a belt around your belly called "truth" and a bulletproof vest on your chest called, "the right thing to do", and a good pair of shoes on your feet and you can carry a shield to shake off the bullets that come. Then you can put a helmet on your head and a sword in your hand called the Bible. This all sounds sorta screwy but what it means is if you live right nobody's gonna knock you down. But you always gotta be on the watch for somebody sneakin' up on you, and always askin' God's help that they don't sneak up on you and knock you down.

Lazy Bums

Idleness (II Thessalonians 3:6-15)

For the love of God don't have nothing to do with lazy no good bums who don't pay no attention to nobody. You know what you supposed to do so why not do it? We didn't ask nothing from

GOD IS BEAUTIFUL, MAN

nobody and we didn't take anything, and we picked up our own tab too. Of course, we would have been glad if you had picked it up and paid for it but we just wanted to show you how it's supposed to be. So, it boils down to this, if you don't work you don't eat. We know there's some that are just lazy no good bums and all they do is mess round with other people's stuff. But what God wants of them is to get on the ball and off the Welfare and earn their own living. But if they don't, don't give up too soon and don't stomp on them or beat them up and think they're your enemy. Instead, make like they're your brother and something real groovy will come out of it.

They All the Same

Show No Partiality (James 2:1-13)

"Give me a break, man," are familiar words to a prison chaplain or anyone else involved with people who are in trouble with the law. They were spoken to me one day by two boys, ages 13 and 14, who had been involved in a purse snatching incident. When I asked, "Why should I help you out?" the first young man said, "Well, you're a preacher. You are supposed to help people and give them a break."

"I thought everybody was supposed to give people breaks," I said.

The boy responded, "Yeah, but you're a

preacher. You're supposed to really do it."

"What about that lady that you 'rolled' a couple of nights ago?"

One of the boys answered, "Aw, she wasn't nothing but a two-bit whore and only got three or four bucks."

I tried to help the boys see that even that "two-bit whore" was a person just as they were. A few days later I talked with them again of treating people as equals, all of whom are entitled to a break. We then read part of the book of James and the boys reworked the story in this manner:

Listen, you guys, you gotta give everybody the same kind of break no matter what. Suppose a guy comes into your pad and he's got all the in stuff on and a big stick pin and the newest chains and then suppose a guy, like a wino, comes into your pad and he's really copped out and his clothes is a mess, whatta you do? Well if you tell the guy that's all hipped up, "Here, have the best seat in the house", and you tell the wino, "Sit on the floor," man, you're a square and you ain't givin' people an even break.

Listen again, you guys, don't you know that sometimes the winos and the beggars and the people on welfare got more faith than all the squares put together? Don't you know that the squares sometimes think you ain't nothin' but dirt, and forget that God loves you too?

You gotta get with it, man! Don't you remember how God said you gotta treat everybody like yourself and that you better love everybody no matter how low down they are, even if they are turned off?

Don't you know if you did that you busted one of God's laws? And you better remember that God ain't gonna give you a break if you don't give somebody else a break. That's the way it works.

Adam and His Wife
A Play About the Garden of Eden (Genesis)

Place: A garden.

ACT 1

GOD: Hey, Adam.

ADAM: Yeah, man?

GOD: You see all this stuff in the garden, Adam?

ADAM: Yes, I sees it.

GOD: Well, it's all yours.

ADAM: Oh, man, that's great! Thanks, God.

GOD: You can eat everything you see in here, except for one thing.

ADAM: What's that, God?

GOD: You see that tree over there?

ADAM: Yeah, I sees it.

GOD: Well, you don't eat that 'cause if you do you're a dead pigeon.

ADAM: OK, I won't touch it.

ACT 2
God's been busy making all kinds of animals, and

he made a woman, too. This is so Adam won't get lonely.

ADAM: Hi, Eve.

EVE: Hi, Adam. What you doin'?

ADAM: Oh, I'm workin' in my garden.

EVE: You gotta take care of all this?

ADAM: Yeah, I gotta take care of the vegetables and the fruits.

EVE: Sounds like a pretty good job, man.

ADAM: Yeah, it is. How do you like all these animals around here?

EVE: Oh, they're pretty good, but I'm scared of that snake over there.

SNAKE: Hey, what she got against me? I ain't such a bad guy. Guess I'll go up and friendly up to her.

EVE: Hey, how come that snake's comin' this way?

SNAKE: Hey, gal. Did God tell you characters not to eat anything outa this here tree?

EVE: Yeah, how come did you know that? God told us we wasn't supposed to eat it.

SNAKE: Aw, go ahead. Try a piece. You know, Eve, if you eat it you'll be pretty clever.

EVE: Oh, really?

SNAKE: Yeah.

EVE: Oh, I don't suppose a little piece will hurt, will it?

SNAKE: Naw, it really won't. Look, Adam's not lookin' right now. Why don't you take a piece and try it?

GOD IS BEAUTIFUL, MAN

EVE: I think I will. Hey, Adam. Look, I just took a bite outa this. It ain't so bad.

ADAM: Oh, think I will.

ACT 3

Adam and Eve are feeling pretty bad about what they done. They are feelin' rotten and lousy inside.

GOD: Adam, where is you?

ADAM: I'm hiding.

GOD: What did you do? Did you eat from that tree?

ADAM: Oh, no, man, not me. It was Eve, she made me do it.

GOD: Eve, what have you got to say for yourself?

EVE: You see that old snake over there? Well, he made me do it and I'm scared of those things.

GOD: Oh, so that's how it is. Hey, snake, you low-down snake, you. From now on you're gonna crawl on your belly every place you go.

EVE: That sounds kinda rough.

ADAM: Oh, shut up.

GOD: OK, you two. You was gonna have things easy. Now you gonna have them rough. From here on you gotta work for everything you get and if you don't work for it you may have to go on the welfare. Now get outa my garden.

ADAM: There, now you see what you did?

EVE: What are you always tryin' to blame me for?

ADAM: I never shoulda got married.

EVE: *(starts crying)* I always get blamed for everything.

Jonah, You're My Man

A Play About Jonah and the Whale (Jonah)

The Place: Down by the city pier.

The Idea for the Play: The city is full of hoods, horsemen, freaks, con artists, loan sharks and people like that. God don't buy that kind of jazz but he don't really wanta wipe 'em out neither so he sets things up to give 'em a jolt. So he picks out Jonah to give 'em the word.

ACT 1

GOD: Jonah, you're my man.

JONAH: I'm your what, God?

GOD: You're gonna be my Reverend.

JONAH: What you want from me? A Reverend?

GOD: That's right, man. I want you to go into the city and tell those cats that they better straighten up or something's gonna happen to them.

JONAH: How come you picked me?

GOD: 'Cause you're a pretty good guy and I want you to do this for me.

JONAH: I don't think I can do it.

GOD: Yes, you can.

JONAH: But I'm scared.

GOD: Oh, I'll help you out.

JONAH: But how can you do that when you ain't even around? I can't even see you. Those other cats sure can't see you either.

GOD: Don't you worry, now. I'll be with you to help you and I think you'll do a pretty good job.

SCENE 2

In the office at the dock.

TICKET MAN: Can I help you?

JONAH: Yep. I wanna ticket for as far away as I can get.

TICKET MAN: Well, you better tell me where you wanna go.

JONAH: I don't care. I just wanna go.

TICKET MAN: That don't help me none, man! Tell me where you wanna go.

JONAH: See that boat out there?

TICKET MAN: Yeah, I see it.

JONAH: Where's it goin'?

TICKET MAN: It's goin' to Egypt.

JONAH: So am I! Gimme a ticket!

TICKET MAN: You got the money?

JONAH: Sure. How much it gonna cost?

TICKET MAN: Fifty bucks. How come you're shakin' so there? You done somethin'?

JONAH: No. I ain't done nothin'. What you askin' me that for?

TICKET MAN: Well, you look like you're scared and you're shakin' all over.

JONAH: Never mind that. Just gimme the ticket. When's the boat leave?

TICKET MAN: In about an hour.

ACT 2

On the ship.

CAPTAIN: Good evening, Jonah.

JONAH: What's good about it?

CAPTAIN: How come you're hangin' over that rail like that?

JONAH: I'm sick, man. I'm awful sick.

CAPTAIN: I think you're gonna get sicker. Looks like there's a big storm comin' up.

JONAH: Thanks a lot, Captain!

SCENE 2

Still on the ship. Big storm outside. All the crew is scared.

CREWMAN 1: Boy, I'm rubbin' my lucky dice here. Maybe that'll make the storm calm down.

CREWMAN 2: I got my rabbit's foot and I'm swinging it around. I think that'll help.

CREWMAN 3: I'm going down and get my lucky quarter. That'll probably fix things up.

CAPTAIN: Hey, you guys. Get up here and help us throw this stuff overboard before we sink.

CREWMAN 1: Oh, look at that guy over there. He's asleep and he don't even know there's a storm.

CAPTAIN: *(Speaking to Jonah)* Get up, man, what's the matter with you, you crazy? What if this ship sinks? You're gonna drown!

Everybody's doin' everything they can and you ain't doin' nothin' to help! Why don't you start prayin', man?

CREWMAN 2: I'll bet somebody's done something rotten and that's why we're in all this mess.

CREWMAN 3: *(Staring at Jonah)* Hey, look at him. He looks kinda funny. Look me in the eye, man and tell me you ain't done nothin'.

JONAH: What you buggin' me for?

CAPTAIN: I got matchsticks here and one's a short one. Everybody take one. Whoever gets the short one, he's the guy that got us in this mess. *(Everybody draws matchsticks.)*

CREWMAN 3: How about that! I told you he was the guy. He's got the short one. What the hell did you do?

JONAH: *(Shaking, 'cause he is really scared now)* I'm runnin' away. God told me to go into the city and get things straightened out and give people the word.

CAPTAIN: What you runnin' away from God for then? And what can we do to stop this storm before we all get killed?

JONAH: Maybe if you throw me overboard and you get rid of me. I'm always causing trouble. You're in this mess only because of me!

CAPTAIN: That sounds kinda spooky. Come on, guys, start rowin'.

CREWMAN 1: The storm's gettin' worse.

CREWMAN 2: Yeah, it is.

CREWMAN 3: Looks like it's him or us!

CAPTAIN: Jonah, man, I don't like to do this but over you go!

CREWMAN 2: Hey, how 'bout that! The storm did cool it! Lookit, there's no more waves!

CAPTAIN: Crazy, man! How 'bout that!

SCENE 3.

Jonah in the water. Swimmin' for mad. Whales not far away.

WHALE: O boy, am I hungry. Wish I could find something to eat. Hey, what's that splashin' over there? Can't figure that out but guess I'll eat it anyway. *Gulp.* Y-a-a-c-k, what was that?

JONAH: Y-e-e-c-h! Where am I? What happened? Somethin' stinks in here.

WHALE: I don't know what I ate but I'm sure gettin' a guts ache!

JONAH: Man, I gotta get outta here! What did I do to get in here, anyway? Oh, yeah, that's it. I bet I'm gettin' this for coppin out on God.

GOD: Now you're beginnin' to understand, huh?

JONAH: Yeah, I got the message now. I'm hearin' it. You're comin' through real good.

GOD: You gonna go in the city now and get those people straightened out?

JONAH: Yes, sir!

WHALE: Man, have I gotta guts ache. I think I'm gonna throw up! Y-e-e-c-h!

JONAH: Wow! How did I get up on this beach?

GOD: Remember me?

JONAH: I sure do!

GOD: You got something to do, man?

JONAH: Yes, sir! I'm goin' right now!

ACT 3

In the city. Jonah's got a big band and he's out on the Mall. After the band plays Jonah starts preaching.

JONAH: All right, childrens. Come on over here. I got things to tell you. I got the word from the Lord. If you guys don't straighten up and stop gettin' charged up and you dealers knockin' it off, your days are done. And if all you cats who wear the in and outer don't get with it you never gonna hit the streets. *(Everybody starts singin' "Hear the Word of the Lord.")*

KING: Now, listen. This cat's right. We gotta straighten up. Nobody's gonna eat, everybody's gonna pray. We're gonna get back on the Lord's side. *(Everybody sings "The Same Boat, Brother.")*

GOD: Good! Old Jonah made 'em hear. I guess I won't bust up the place after all.

JONAH: I told them that this place was gonna get busted up and you ain't done nothing. So what I said didn't come true. I'm gonna lose face. I wish I was dead.

GOD: Oh, that's stupid, Jonah. You did what I wanted you to do. Now everything's OK.

SCENE 2

Just outside the city Jonah builds a shack to sit in so he can watch and see what might happen.

JONAH: *(Sitting in booth)* Hey, how come? There's a grapevine growin'. Man, that thing's growin' fast! That's kinda funny! Real spooky! Oh, well, it's a good thing. Give me some shade. I don't care.

(Next day)

JONAH: Hey, look. That vine that grew so fast yesterday is dyin'. Oh, boy, that sun's gonna come in here and, wow, is that wind blowin'. Oh, this heat's awful! Aw, I'd be better off dead.

GOD: Hey, Jonah. What you gripin' about?

JONAH: I had some nice shade and now it's gone.

GOD: So OK. You get bugged out 'cause that vine's all gone in a day. How do you think those cats in the city would feel if their houses was all busted up?

JONAH: Oh, I get it. *(People in city start singing "Where Have All the Flowers Gone?")*

A Christmas Play

This Christmas play was developed by a group of six children between the ages of 12 and 14. In preparation, for the project, I showed them the filmstrip, "Christopher Mouse," and read them

GOD IS BEAUTIFUL, MAN

the Christmas story in Matthew's and Luke's gospels. Stories about the writing of "Silent Night" and "O Little Town of Bethlehem" were also read to them. These three steps were taken over a period of one week. At appropriate times I began to plant the seed for the play by commenting, "I wonder what it would be like if Christ were born today in our city." Initially, puzzled looks were the only response. A boy finally said, "He couldn't be. We ain't got no stables any more." Another boy's response was, "I don't dig those shepherds and wise men. Who the hell were they anyway?" This remark opened a discussion about who the shepherds really were, and one youngster exclaimed, "You mean like neighbors who really care about you?" This seemed to me to be as close as we could get to the real meaning of the shepherds.

The next step was to define the wise men in current terms that would touch the lives of the participants. We discussed kings, but their concept of a king was of someone whom they had seen in a movie, a man who was always at war. They did not see a king as one who expressed interest and concern in another person. One of the boys brought up the term "wheels". We discovered that the biggest wheels in his block were the block club officers, who usually knew what was going on in the area and who were turned to when neighborhood people needed help. Thus we seemed to have a close equivalent to the meaning of "wise men".

At about this point in our discussions, I suggested that we try writing a play about Christmas. With the information that had been given to the children about Christmas and the hint, through the use of the filmstrip, that the Christmas story could be seen through different eyes, we were ready to begin. But what would be the setting? Someone had already pointed out that there were no stables. The suggestion came, "Why not in an apartment, even if they have to squeeze in with somebody?" From that point, imaginations ran wild, and needed occasional mild restraint.

So the play is the result of many hours of work and minimal guidance, with the objective of conveying the basic idea of Christmas in terms and concepts meaningful to inner city youth. A secondary purpose was to provide a base for communicating the real meaning of the Incarnation of Christ, the concern of one human being for another, and especially the concern and love of God for all His children.

Cool Yule

Place: Any block in the center of a large city. This play can be given in the chancel of a church, on the stage of a settlement house, or in similar settings. If scenery is possible, have a very simply furnished room, preferably with cracked plaster or holes in the wall. The furniture should be only

GOD IS BEAUTIFUL, MAN

slightly dilapidated, the suggestion should be of borderline poverty. In place of a cradle or crib have a simple box. Costumes should consist of contemporary clothing, slightly worn and some characters should have clothing just a little too large for them. The Christ child should be wrapped in a simple blanket. Christmas music such as "Calypso Carol" or "White Christmas" may be played in the background over a small table radio. Mary is lying on a couch; Joseph is standing holding the baby.

JOSEPH: Look, Mary, it's a boy!

MARY: Gee, that's wonderful! *(She reaches for the child. There is a knock on the door.)*

JOSEPH: Now who's that? *(Goes to the door offstage, comes back to Mary.)*

JOSEPH: Mary, all the neighbors have come. They knew you were gonna have a baby and they said it seemed like they heard voices telling them to come over to our apartment.

MARY: Well, tell them to come in.

(Neighbors enter.)

FIRST NEIGHBOR: My, don't he look like his mother?

SECOND NEIGHBOR: That's a real pretty blanket you got on him.

THIRD NEIGHBOR: He looks real cute and pretty there in the box.

FIRST NEIGHBOR: You hear that, Mary, hear that pretty music? Seems like we just had to come and see your baby.

MARY: That's nice.

FIRST NEIGHBOR: We were all over in another apartment havin' a cup of coffee.

SECOND NEIGHBOR: Yeah, and the lights went dim like and then got real bright.

FIRST NEIGHBOR: Shook us up, too!

THIRD NEIGHBOR: Then it seemed like a voice was speakin' right outta the walls. Tellin' us not to be scared 'cause a real great kid had been born.

FOURTH NEIGHBOR: And it almost seemed we heard a voice saying that the kid would be lying in a box. The only one we knew that was gonna have a baby was you, Mary, so that's why we is here.

FIRST NEIGHBOR: We shoulda had a shower for you, Mary, but we didn't have enough money to get presents. The only thing I got to give the kid anyway is my cigarette lighter. Maybe he can use it when he grows up.

SECOND NEIGHBOR: I don't have very much either, Mary, but I'd sure like to give him somethin'. Why don't you take this here scarf of mine? Maybe you can wrap it around his head when you take him outdoors.

THIRD NEIGHBOR: Mary, my kid's got two pairs of mittens and I got one pair in my pocket, so I'm givin' them to you and you can put them on the kid's hands when he goes out.

MARY: Thanks a lot. I sure can use all this stuff.

FIRST NEIGHBOR: Looks to me like there's somethin' special about that kid. Maybe he'll grow up and be a real wheel some day.

(There is a knock on the door. First Neighbor goes to the door and yells back:)

FIRST NEIGHBOR: It's Larry. *(Larry comes in carrying a little puppy.)*

LARRY: Did Mary have her kid?

FIRST NEIGHBOR: She sure did. There it is, sleeping in the box.

LARRY: *(Goes over and kneels before the box.)* What a cute kid. I brought you a puppy. Hope you like him.

MARY: Gee, that was awful nice of you.

LARRY: There's a bunch of kids out in the street wanta come in and see the baby too. You know, Mary and Joseph, it's a funny thing—the whole neighborhood knows you got this baby! And everybody's got an idea there's somethin' special about this kid. What is it?

JOSEPH: Maybe he is gonna grow up and be president some day. But I think the neighborhood kids better wait till morning. Mary's kinda tired and we don't want to wake the kid up till his two o'clock feeding.

MARY: Oh, it's alright, Joe. Why don't you let 'em come in, and take a quick look? *(First Neighbor and Larry go over and let some children in.)*

FIRST CHILD: Gee, ain't he nice.

SECOND CHILD: Yeah, man.

THIRD CHILD: Get outta my way, I want to see him.

FIRST CHILD: Mrs. Mary, I brought your baby a present. Maybe he can use this little truck.

SECOND CHILD: Look, I brought him a ball.

THIRD CHILD: Here's like a bird that I made over at the settlement house.

FIRST CHILD: I got a piece of candy here if he wants it.

SECOND CHILD: How about a piece of gum?

FOURTH CHILD: *(Small one who has been in the background.)* Hey, ain't I gonna get to see the baby?

(Joseph picks up the Fourth Child, holds him on his knee so the small child can look in the box to see the baby.)

FOURTH CHILD: Ain't he nice.

FIRST CHILD: Why don't you keep your mouth shut? Look, you woke him up.

SECOND CHILD: Maybe we can sing him to sleep. *(Children sing "Silent Night.")*

FIRST CHILD: *(Softly)* How come you got him in a box?

SECOND CHILD: Yeah, how come the whole neighborhood is comin' over here?

THIRD CHILD: Mary, some day can I hold him?

FIRST CHILD: Look, I got a flower that the man down at the funeral home gave me.

MARY: Oh, that's a very pretty rose.

FIRST CHILD: Yeah, I think I'll give it to your baby, Mary.

JOSEPH: You better not. It's got prickers on it.

MARY: No, it ain't got no prickers.

JOSEPH: What's that? Seems like I heard a couple of cars stop out front of the house. Wait'll I go look out the window. *(Comes back)* It's all the officers from the block club. Wonder what they want? I'd better go let them in.

(The President, vice-president, and secretary of the block club enter.)

PRESIDENT: We came to see your baby. Seems like we heard a voice telling us to come see him. And anyway, it seemed like all the lights were brightest and a real funny pull inside of me told me I'd better come see the baby.

FIRST NEIGHBOR: Ain't that funny? We got the same feeling.

VICE PRESIDENT: Gee, that's one of the nicest babies I have ever seen!

SECRETARY: Mary, I just had to come. Nothing could keep me away. I brought you this present which I want you to give to the baby, Mary. It's just a little something from my whole family.

PRESIDENT: Everything seems so peaceful around here. Wonder what it is?

VICE PRESIDENT: Maybe some of the prayers that we been sayin' is gonna get answered. You know, just for a little bit of peace.

MARY: There's nothing like a little baby to make things feel all right, is there?

SECOND NEIGHBOR: You can say that again, Mary.

PRESIDENT: Mary, I don't have very much but I want you to take this buck and buy somethin' real nice for your baby.

VICE PRESIDENT: I got some stuff here, Mary, I got it down to the little department store. You put it in a dish and light it and the whole house will smell good.

MARY: Everybody is bein' so nice to me and we got more stuff than we ever had before. Maybe there is somethin' real special about my baby.

PRESIDENT: We sure dreamed and talked about somebody to help us get out of all these messes and we all feel so good inside right now that maybe it really is true that this baby came right from God.

FIRST CHILD: Wow!

SECOND CHILD: Ain't that cool!

THIRD CHILD: Yeah, groovy!

FIRST NEIGHBOR: He better look out or everybody will spoil him before he even grows up.

VICE PRESIDENT: I don't think so. Because if he came from God nobody can do him any dirt.

SECRETARY: You know that old troublemaker down the block. The one that's always stirrin' up things. He was askin' me what all the fuss in the neighborhood was about.

PRESIDENT: We better not tell him about this baby.

VICE PRESIDENT: Yeah, when we go home we better go around the block and he won't even know we been here.

SECRETARY: Well, I think we better get goin'. Maybe Mary needs to get some sleep. *(Block club officers leave.)*

FIRST NEIGHBOR: Yeah, I think you are right. Come on, kids, let's all go home now and then we can come back tomorrow and see how things are goin'. *(Neighbors and children quietly leave.)*

MARY: Wasn't that nice of everybody to come?

JOSEPH: Yeah, it sure was. *(Joseph picks up the baby and sings "Sweet Little Jesus Boy." At conclusion he turns to Mary.)* Kinda hard to keep this place warm in the winter, Mary. Why don't we take the baby over to my mother's house. It's warmer there.

MARY: Well, I kinda hate to leave the house and all the neighbors and the block club officers have been so good to us.

JOSEPH: But I got a funny feelin' that somethin' may happen to the baby if we don't get out of here. Maybe he'll catch pneumonia or somethin'.

MARY: Well, you're the boss man if you think that's what we ought to do, then maybe we better do it. *(Radio comes back on playing "O Holy Night.")*

Glossary

Bag: concern, interest
Bested: got the better of
Blast: party
Bopping: fighting
Bread: money
Broad: girl or woman
Bug: bother, to give trouble
Can it: take it easy, calm down
Cat: boy or man
Chew out: scold, yell at
Chicken: scared
Climb on: start a fight
Con artist: good talker
Contract: an agreement to kill someone
Cool: calm, easy
Cop out: to give up, not accept responsibility
Crib: home
Freak out: lose his mind
Gas: meaningless words
Get proved: willingness to fight
Go up on: to fight
Groovy: good, OK
Hang the bag on: blame
Heart: willingness to fight
Hep: wise, or knowledgeable
Hip: excited
Hipes: drug addicts
Heist: steal
Jammed up: worried, concerned
Jerk: despised person
Joint: prison
Joker: despised person

Knock it off: stop

Kook: person whose views differ

Low boil: quick to anger

Man: almost anyone, a term for emphasis

Mano: Spanish version of "man"

Mr. Big: important person

Piece: weapon

Prez: president of a gang

Pross: prostitute

Pad: home territory

Rub out: remove a person

Rumble: fight

Snow job: group of lies

Spooked: scared, upset

Stoned: drunk

Teach': teacher

Teed off: angry

Turf: home

Wheel: important person

Wino: an alcoholic